NEW YEATS PAPERS XII

1. Design by Victor Brown from *A Broadside*, No. 3 (New Series), March 1937, edited by Dorothy Wellesley and W. B. Yeats. The drawing illustrates the poem 'Lass, is your heart dead?' by Dorothy Wellesley. It is reproduced by courtesy of the Directors of the Cuala Press (see p. 55).

EDWARD O'SHEA

YEATS AS EDITOR

THE DOLMEN PRESS

CONTENTS

Introduction	*page* 5
Yeats as Editor	
I Irish Editions 1888-1906	9
II Dun Emer and The Cuala Press	36
III The Oxford Book of Modern Verse	57
Appendix: Suggested additions to Wade's *Bibliography*	73
Notes on the text	74

ILLUSTRATIONS

1. 'Lass, is your heart dead?', from *A Broadside*, March 1937	frontispiece
2. *Fairy and Folk Tales of the Irish Peasantry*, 1888	*page* 8
3. *The Works of William Blake*, 1893	29
4. *Beltaine*, No. 1, 1899	33
5. *Samhain*, No. 1, 1901	34
6. *Selections from the Writings of Lord Dunsany*, 1912	44
7. *The Oxford Book of Modern Verse*, 1936	61

General Editor: Liam Miller

Yeats material quoted © Anne and Michael Yeats.
© Edward O'Shea 1975   ISBN 0 85105 276 2

Printed and published in the Republic of Ireland at the Dolmen Press, North Richmond Industrial Estate, North Richmond Street, Dublin 1.
First published 1975.
Distributed in the United States of America and in Canada by Humanities Press Inc., 171 First Avenue, Atlantic Highlands, N.J. 07716.

INTRODUCTION

W. B. Yeats was not an impartial scholarly editor and this fact explains in part the fascination of his editions. This does not mean that his edited work has no value other than what it tells us about Yeats the poet. The Yeats-Ellis edition of William Blake's poetry, for example, is an important, though eccentric contribution to Blake studies and would stand by itself even if Yeats had never come into his own as a poet.

But given the fact that Yeats did become a poet of stature, his editions deserve attention if only because he put so much of his energy into them. His *Fairy and Folk Tales of the Irish Peasantry* (1888) coincides with his first fully creative work, and as late as 1935, long after Yeats had ceased to depend on his edited work as a major source of income, he was working long hours reading and sifting for *The Oxford Book of Modern Verse*. In between was Yeats's long task as editor of the Dun Emer and the Cuala Press and the publications of the Irish theatre.

Yeats's editing was an important means of acting on the life around him, an aspect of Yeats's longing to be a 'man of action' as well as a poet (though in his poem 'The Choice' he says the two are not compatible). His editions were a principal method for advancing Yeats's numerous enthusiasms, whether for a national literature in 1888, a return to heroic exulting poetry in 1936, or for individual poets such as Oliver Gogarty.

Yeats did not believe that an editor should be a discrete impersonal arbiter of what constituted the best text of one of his authors. As likely as not, if he thought an improvement could be made, and if an author was at all pliant — or dead, he made it himself. Behind this practice was Yeats's belief that genius or talent was a kind of common resource that all creative people drew on collectively. If he could help a young writer because of his own long experience as a poet, he would do so, just as he had been helped himself by his editors and as poets historically had helped each other. 'It has always been done in a company of poets,' he explained to Dorothy Wellesley when she baulked at his revisions of her poetry.

Yeats's revisions of other writers, poets especially, were guided by a few constant principles. Chief of these is the 'integrity of traditional forms' and it can be illustrated by Yeats's revisions of other writers at the beginning and end of his life, initially by his insistence that the folk tale be left to interpret itself, and finally by his requirement that the ballad keep a naive spontaneity devoid of philosophizing or moralizing. At other times, he might give the kind of general advice expected of any good editor; he worked for a living language, a suppression of 'the words that have not got their souls yet and the words that have lost their souls,' as Tagore formulated the lesson he had learned from Yeats, also directness of statement and narrative economy in poetry. Jon Stallworthy has noted that in revising his own poetry, Yeats worked from fullness to concentration, cutting rather than adding material. In revising the work of others, Yeats usually followed this same practice, deleting lines or whole stanzas to achieve homogeneity or a single effect.

Yeats was continuously accused by his critics of having an eye only for poetry that was like his own. As Stephen Spender said of Yeats while reviewing *The Oxford Book of Modern Verse* in 1936, 'Great poet as he himself is, he seems from among his contemporaries, definitely to prefer that which is either second rate or else a pale imitation of his own manner.' Certainly many of the poets Yeats promoted in his editions were 'minor', to use a more neutral term. But while it is true that Yeats was attracted to poets who substantiated his own themes, it is just as true that he had little time for his mindless imitators, and his editions taken all together testify to this.

While Yeats can be said to have edited his own work, this is not the subject of this study. It is rather Yeats's editions of other writers. 'Edit' is a general term. In deciding what is a Yeats edition, I have looked for three things: that Yeats chose a subject or author for publication, that he had some control over selecting contents, that he revised or in some way altered the edited material from its original form. (This last criterion would seem strange in a contemporary description of 'editing', but it applies to Yeats.) These tests are not always applied rigorously or in concert; in the 1890's (and later) Yeats did not always choose the subjects of his editions, but a book such as *Irish Fairy Tales* shows the Yeats stamp very clearly anyway. Nor did Yeats invariably alter material he edited. Within these guidelines, there are still degrees of editorial endeavour, and it is often difficult to determine Yeats's exact contribution to a particular edition. This is especially true of some of the volumes from the Dun Emer and Cuala Press for which Yeats was general editorial advisor. This may explain why Wade's *Bibliography*, invaluable as it is, is incomplete in its listing of Yeats's editions. It omits, for example, the work of Dorothy Wellesley and Rabindranath Tagore that Yeats edited. *Gitanjali* and *Selections from the Poetry of Dorothy Wellesley* did not specifically name Yeats as editor, but they are his editions in a fuller sense than, for example, the later *Samhain* which Wade lists (rightly) under Yeats's edited work. This brief study cannot hope to treat all of Yeats's editions, but the reader should be warned that to determine what is a Yeats edition requires more than a glance at title pages.

ACKNOWLEDGEMENTS

Acknowledgement is given:

To Anne and Michael B. Yeats for permission to quote previously unpublished letters, inscriptions, and annotations of W. B. Yeats;

To the Delegates of the Oxford University Press for permission to quote material from their file for *The Oxford Book of Modern Verse*;

To Macmillan & Co. Ltd.

To The Henry W. and Albert A. Berg Collection, Astor, Lenox and Tilden Foundations, The New York Public Library;

The Harvard College Library;

The National Library of Ireland;

for permission to quote or make use of material in their collections.

FAIRY AND FOLK TALES
OF THE IRISH PEASANTRY:
EDITED AND SELECTED BY
W. B. YEATS.

LONDON
WALTER SCOTT, 24 WARWICK LANE
NEW YORK: THOMAS WHITTAKER
TORONTO: W. J. GAGE AND CO.
1888

2. Title page: *Fairy and Folk Tales of the Irish Peasantry*, 1888.

YEATS AS EDITOR

I IRISH EDITIONS 1888-1900, BLAKE AND SPENSER

I

W. B. Yeats assumed the role of editor only insofar as it was another literary odd job, though one that interested him more than journalism. His first edited volume was *Fairy and Folk Tales of the Irish Peasantry*, published in 1888 when he was twenty-three.[1] Yeats says of this collection that it cost him more than three months' reading for which he was paid only twelve pounds, 'but I did not think myself badly paid for I had chosen the work for my own purposes': while earning his money, he hoped to study 'the tradition of Ireland.'[2] One of the authors in this tradition was T. Crofton Croker, nineteenth century Irish antiquarian, folklorist and humorist, and *Fairy and Folk Tales* began in Yeats's mind as a reprinting of Croker's *Fairy Legends and Traditions of the South of Ireland* (*Letters*, 45). It soon grew to a more ambitious collection.

While Croker was well represented in *Fairy and Folk Tales* by twelve tales, Yeats added selections by William Carleton, Lady Wilde and a good number of lesser known collectors of folk tales, as well as three stories 'from the Irish' by a promising new writer, Douglas Hyde. Yeats also included poetry — his own, William Allingham's, Samuel Ferguson's and more, as well as a short introduction, transitional material and notes (for which he had the help of Hyde). *Fairy and Folk Tales* is thus more Yeats's own book than a simple reprinting from Croker would have been. But Yeats the editor has imposed his own viewpoint on this book in a way that goes beyond the mere selection and arrangement of material.

Yeats had written to Katharine Tynan from London in March of 1888: 'Fairies are not popular this side of the water, are considered unscientific' (*Letters*, 62). Some months later, while working on *Fairy and Folk Tales* and while contemplating 'a series of articles on the difference between Scotch and Irish fairies,' he wrote Miss Tynan again: 'All will go well if I can keep my own unpopular thoughts out of them [the articles]. To be mechanical and workmanlike is at present my deepest ambition. I must be careful in no way to suggest that fairies, or something like do veritably exist . . .' (*Letters*, 96-7). In his Introduction to *Fairy and Folk Tales* Yeats approached this same subject circumspectly: 'The reader will perhaps wonder that in all my notes I have not rationalised a single hobgoblin. I seek for shelter to the words of Socrates.'[3] He then quotes (from *Phaedrus*) Socrates's reply on being asked if he believed the tale of Boreas and Orithyia: 'to be curious about that which is not my business, while I am still in ignorance of my own self, would be ridiculous. And therefore, I say farewell to all this; the common opinion is enough for me.' Yet, though Yeats had not 'rationalised a single hobgoblin', this cannot be easily said of all those Irish writers whose tales he included in *Fairy and Folk Tales*.

While Yeats notes approvingly that collectors of Irish folklore 'made their work literature rather than science,'[4] the writers from whom he borrowed his fairy tales for *Fairy and Folk Tales* were quite often apologetic and condescending towards them, and this he could not sanction. The note of apology is expressed perhaps most ingenuously by Patrick Kennedy in the Preface to his *Legendary Fictions of the Irish Celts*, a collection that Yeats drew on extensively for *Fairy and Folk Tales*:

> If a fastidious reader fails to take pleasure or interest in the mere tales, and experiences contempt for the taste of those ancestors of ours who could have relished them so much as they evidently did, perhaps he may be induced to search into the history, and the polity, and the social usages of those easily-pleased folk, and discover the cause of their want of critical acumen. In this case the acquisition of archaeological knowledge, more or less, will recompense the time lost in the perusal of a mere FOLK'S BOOK.[5]

Though Kennedy undervalued his folk sources, he had at least a genuine concern for their survival, and as Yeats comments, 'seems to have had a something of genuine belief in the fairies.'[6] The same cannot be said of the author of 'Superstitions of the Irish Peasantry' which appeared serially in *The Dublin and London Magazine* beginning in March 1825. Yeats included one story from this serial in *Fairy and Folk Tales*, 'Loughleagh (Lake of Healing).'[7]

The anonymous transcriber of 'Superstitions of the Irish Peasantry' introduced his series authoritatively:

> It is a singular fact, in the history of the human mind, that man will embrace any doctrine, however absurd, rather than continue in doubt; for nothing can be more irritating than a novel or strange effect without any assignable cause. Hence superstition is the consequence of imperfect knowledge; for when men, in the infancy of the sciences, were unable to account, on natural principles, for the daily phenomena which took place around them, they attributed what they could not comprehend to the agency of aerial beings, whom their imagination invested with peculiar powers; both good and evil.[8]

It seems probable that Yeats would have read this while searching out material for *Fairy and Folk Tales*. It is more certain that he would have disagreed with it, but he could afford to ignore it, for the excerpt he chose from the serial 'Superstitions of the Irish Peasantry', 'Loughleagh (Lake of Healing)' was presented in a straightforward manner, without sceptical intrusion and could be easily isolated from its offensive introduction. Certain of the other stories collected in *Fairy and Folk Tales* presented slightly more difficulty, since disparagement of the fairies was included in the actual tale. Yeats's solution was to silently revise many of the offending pieces. Such was the case with a number of Carleton's stories.

William Carleton is best known for his novels and stories of rural Irish life in the nineteenth century rather than as a collector of folklore. This does him little injustice, for as Douglas Hyde says of his folk tales, they are 'incidental and largely-manipulated.'[9] Yeats himself in the Introduction to *Fairy and Folk Tales* admits that of Carleton's many stories, he was able to include only 'a few of the slightest.' One of these is 'Frank Martin and the Fairies', but Yeats's version is some eight pages shorter than that found in Carleton's 1869 collection called *The Poor Scholar and Other Tales*.[10] The eight pages that Yeats has cut from his version (unacknowledged) are no loss at all — any editor given the opportunity would have done the same, for they delay the story of Frank Martin interminably with, among other things, a three page fever-induced dispute between Carleton's right foot and left foot over a matter of precedence. But Yeats was enforcing more than narrative integrity in his exclusion, for Carleton's initial pages are a sustained attack on 'the absurd doctrine of apparitions.' [11]

Carleton here is not at his most attractive or lucid, and his argument is a pseudo-logical statement which takes note of the basic similarities of folk tales among different racial groups, only to suggest that the *differences* of detail are the most telling, for 'If these inane bugbears possessed the consistence of truth and reality, their appearance to mankind would be always uniform, unchangeable, and congruous; but they are beheld, so to speak, through different prejudices and impressions, and consequently change with the media through which they are seen.' [12] Yeats, in his version of 'Frank Martin', omits Carleton's initial and final rationalization, 'that great sin against art',[13] as he calls it, leaving the tale to explain itself.

It is quite possible that Carleton, by rationalizing the supernatural element in 'Frank Martin', was only trying to make his tale more acceptable to his audience — largely the same English audience Yeats had reminded himself of in his letter to Katharine Tynan ('Fairies are not popular this side of the water'). But the 'language of explanation' which Thomas Flanagan suggests is an abiding quality of nineteenth century Irish fiction is no more palatable for the reason that it is meant to interpret Irish life to an English reading public.[14] It gives Carleton's tale a lack of integration which Yeats, with his greater belief, could only deplore (and suppress).

Carleton is not the only author whose work in *Fairy and Folk Tales* is reshaped through Yeats's editing. Some of this reshaping would be uncontroversial under almost any editorial policy. Yeats, for example, removes transitional passages from Lady Wilde's 'The Demon Cat' and Croker's 'The Brewery of Egg-Shells', providing his own apparatus to replace them. In other tales by these same authors, passages seem to be cut because they are merely transitional or irrelevant, but on closer examination there are other elements in them which Yeats might be expected to object to and therefore remove. This is what he has done with a passage in Lady Wilde's 'The Priest's Soul' where she sees an 'ethical purpose' in the story of the priest who becomes so wise that he denies heaven, hell, and his own soul. There is an obvious moral to this tale, but it is unnecessary to emphasize it.

In the Introduction to *Fairy and Folk Tales* Yeats treats T. Crofton Croker and Samuel Lover together as examples of a vital but flawed approach to Irish folklore:

> Croker and Lover, full of the ideas of harum-scarum Irish gentility, saw everything humorised. The impulse of the Irish literature of their time came from a class that did not — mainly for political reasons—take the populace seriously, and imagined the country as a humorist's Arcadia; its passion, its gloom, its tragedy, they knew nothing of. What they did was not wholly false; they merely magnified an irresponsible type, found oftenest among boatmen, carmen, and gentlemen's servants, into the type of a whole nation, and created the stage Irishman. . . . Their work had the dash as well as the shallowness of an ascendant and idle class. . . .[15]

Of the selections that Yeats has made from Lover in *Fairy and Folk Tales*, this 'humorist's Arcadia' is perhaps most clearly seen in a piece called 'King O'Toole and His Goose', or more accurately in Lover's original story 'King O'Toole and St. Kevin', for Yeats's version is a virtual rewriting of that tale. In Lover's original, the account of how St. Kevin rehabilitated King O'Toole's favourite diversion, his goose, is told by a guide, Joe Irwin, to a nameless interlocutor, obviously a relatively sophisticated and sceptical member of the Irish gentry. Inherent in this device is a certain diminishment of Joe Irwin and a distancing of *his* tale, for the reader is invited into the gentleman's confidence as he faults Irwin's historical accuracy (Churches did not exist in King O'Toole's time) or suppresses his amusement with Joe and his tale ('Here an involuntary smile was produced by this regal mode of recreation, "the royal game of goose" ').[16] Since Yeats's intention is obviously to make Joe Irwin, who is recounting the legend, less of a stage Irishman, he suppresses the interlocutor and rewrites the story more impersonally (Irwin is not mentioned by name), removing some of the dialect along the way. To make the tale itself more respectable, he also pares down a passage where the King and Saint greet each other redundantly as if they were two senile old men, at another point suppresses some of Kevin's saintly abhorrence of money, and cuts a long description of the regenerated goose flying over the landmarks of Ireland. This last epic digression might offer untold possibilities for the storyteller's embellishment, but for the modern reader, it is a bothersome diversion. Yeats's reshaping of 'King O'Toole and St. Kevin', though it softens the buffoonery and makes the tale more narratively direct, does retain the vitality and colour of the language and the legitimate humour that are the story's real virtues.

It should be clear by now that to label *Fairy and Folk Tales* a casual and make-work collection of stories belies the evidence of a strong personality at work. Though Yeats was only twenty-three, he had very definite ideas about the Irish folk tale as an artistic form. If there is one concept which encompasses these ideas and points to a principle for Yeats's future editions, it is that of 'generic integrity'. Yeats in *Fairy and Folk Tales* demands of the authors he collects that they take the folk tale seriously (not merely as a vehicle for the stage Irishman), that they not denigrate the form or its assumptions (the inexplicable should not be explained), and that they should tell their tale directly without unnecessary digressions or qualifications. Admittedly his authors as a group were a rather fractious lot, but his solution to Carleton's ponderous scepticism, Lady Wilde's sermonizing, or Lover's superior gentleman was what Yeats considered the editor's prerogative, the bold slash and the discrete rewrite. None of his authors objected (most were dead).

Yeats returned to the fairies in a volume for 'The Children's Library', *Irish Fairy Tales* published in 1892. It was in a way a more modest version of *Fairy and Folk Tales*, and while it duplicates none of the selections in the earlier book, the authors are much the same, with the addition of P. W. Joyce, Gerald Griffin, and Standish O'Grady. The apparatus is also similar, a short introduction, an appendix classifying the Irish fairies (drawn from an earlier article in *Lucifer*), and another on 'Authorities On Irish Folklore'.[17]

The format of *Irish Fairy Tales* then is similar to *Fairy and Folk Tales*, and Yeats's editorial policy too remains the same. A good number of these stories have been cut or reworked in some way, for the same reasons as were those in his earlier collection. For example, Yeats has removed a long but inoffensive preamble to the main story of Carleton's 'The Rival Kempers' and has done the same to a shorter introduction to Lady Wilde's 'Seanchan the Bard and the King of the Cats'. Samuel Lover's two stories, 'The Devil's Mill' and 'The Little Weaver of Duleek Gate' have been cut and slightly rewritten to remove the device of the interlocutor, in the first piece a painter whose superiority to the narrator is particularly offensive. Even Standish O'Grady's 'Knighting of Cuchulain' has been reduced by three pages to accent the main action. Finally, P. W. Joyce's 'Fergus O'Mara and the Air Demons' has been shortened by one paragraph, removing a moral tag in which Fergus O'Mara amends his life by getting to Mass 'before the rest of the congregation had started from their homes.'[18]

As he was often to do later, Yeats made his reading for *Fairy and Folk Tales* do double-duty. By May of 1889 he was adding to what he already knew of Carleton for a volume in The Scott Library. *Stories from Carleton* (1889) includes six stories, all taken from Carleton's *Traits and Stories of the Irish Peasantry*. This selection presented some difficulties. Yeats divided Carleton's work into three periods. The first dates from Carleton's conversion to Protestantism in 1818 and includes a great deal of anti-Catholic propaganda as he came under the influence of Caesar Otway and *The Christian Examiner*. While Yeats considered the fiction of this period to be better than the historical novels of Carleton's final 'twenty years' decadence', he thought it inferior to his middle work.[19] *Traits and Stories* belongs to the first period; nevertheless the stories contained there were relatively short and easy to excerpt. This suited Yeats's purpose, because in making *Stories from Carleton* he was under a tighter than usual deadline (*Letters*, 130). The simplicity of reprinting a number of *Traits and Stories* rather than excerpting the novels must have been the deciding factor. Nevertheless, there remained the problem of Carleton's anti-Catholic bias in this early work.

Yeats should have been forewarned through his correspondence with Fr. Matthew Russell, the editor of the *Irish Monthly*, that Carleton, though twenty years dead, was a potentially explosive author. Fr. Russell had apparently objected to Carleton's anti-clericalism; Yeats countered with the observation that Carleton had been equally severe with the Protestant clergy, that he had, after all, included some admirable priests in his fiction, and that his anti-Catholic period was a youthful episode of a few years. But he adds an important concession, 'Unhappily the *Traits and Stories* was written in those years' (*Letters*, 130-1).

Yeats's solution to a potentially troublesome bias on the part of his Irish readers was to choose carefully from *Traits and Stories*. He avoided the more sensational depictions of Catholic popular practice in Ireland, such as 'The Lough Derg Pilgrim',[20] and settled for some pleasant if boisterous pieces. So he must have thought 'Shane Fadh's Wedding', but as it turned out it was to be a peg on which were hung all of the Catholic indictments against Carleton.

In attendance at Shane Fadh's wedding were Fathers Corrigan and Dollard, later joined by Friar Rooney. Interspersed with the festivities is a progressively more drunken dispute between the two 'seculars' and the friar over the superiority of their way of life to the mendicant's. Charges of clerical abuse are exchanged from both directions, there is a debate in 'bog-Latin', and the priests are last seen dancing with the girls at the wedding party, finally accepting pullets and whiskey as offerings from the parishioners.[21] It should be said of Carleton's story that the priests and the friar are not treated apart from the other participants at this country wedding. If the peasants are a rough group (and Carleton's own origins were here), so are the priests, and it seems natural that they should be.

The reviewer of *Stories from Carleton* in the Dublin newspaper *The Nation* thought otherwise. After quoting a long passage from 'Shane Fadh's Wedding' describing the priests and the friar, it concluded that this was 'envenomed caricature' and that 'the slanderous Carleton should be kept by Irish critics in the literary pillory.'[22] Yeats's reply (in a letter to the editor of *The Nation* on 11 January 1890) defends Carleton in an argument similar to that used with the more liberal Fr. Russell.

Yeats argues that 'Shane Fadh's Wedding', a story of 'almost

Chaucerian breadth and power' was written in a period when Carleton was especially impressionable to the predominant Protestant literature, that he had changed his religion honestly, and that this period had lasted for only a few years. He further asserts that Carleton had made amends by gradually cutting proselytizing passages as his works from this period were republished, and that in fact many had not been republished at all, although they might have been financially profitable. He accuses critics and reviewers of ignoring 'the entirely Catholic' work of his best years — he mentions *The Black Prophet* and *The Emigrants of Ahadarra* — to concentrate on his 'offensive' partisan period. Yeats concludes that, though the Catholic critics might try to 'pillory' Carleton, it was not within their power to prevent the Irish peasantry from revering his memory and talent, and in this he rested satisfied.[23] Privately, in a letter to Katharine Tynan two days after his protest to *The Nation*, Yeats conceded that the objection to Carleton was not altogether a matter of bigotry, but that the anti-Catholic label on Carleton had been uncritically perpetuated for so long that potential readers had naively accepted it as true and had not read his books (*Letters*, 147). Yeats's intention was obviously to win over these readers to Carleton.

Yeats reflected on his edition of Carleton and added a triumphant postscript to the *Nation* controversy in an inscription in Lady Gregory's copy of *Stories from Carleton* made in 1901:

> A good collection I think, but one or other of the pathetic stories should have gone out to make room for "The Geography of an Irish Oath," a masterpiece with a mood of Balzac in it at the outset. I had a controversy about Carleton in "The Nation" when the book came out. Somebody said he was anti-catholic and wrote a long letter. A friar in "Shane Fadh's Wedding" came into the controversy I think. I heard afterwards that a man in the office said he knew just such a friar in Connaught.[24]

Yeats's next edited work, *Representative Irish Tales* (1891), a hastily executed anthology of nineteenth century Irish novelists for Putnam's, the American publisher, included Carleton and nine other authors in two volumes. As was so often the case when Yeats anthologized, he immersed himself in the subject, reading 'innumerable good and bad novels' while making his selection.[25] Not surprisingly, this forced march through Irish fiction left him vulnerable on a number of fronts, one of which was the accuracy of his edition.

Yeats applied to Fr. Russell for suggestions to expand his reading list of Irish authors, and it was to him he explained his rationale for *Representative Irish Tales*: 'I am trying to make all the stories illustrative of some phase of Irish life, meaning the collection to be a kind of social history. I . . . give mainly tales that contain some special kind of Irish humour or tragedy' (*Letters*, 143). Yeats wanted to make a representative selection, but it was on this very point that he was later criticized. It was a familiar objection by now — it had been made to *Fairy and Folk Tales*, to *Stories from Carleton*, and was to be made again to *Irish Fairy Tales* a year later (in 1892) and to work edited much later. The Irish form of the accusation came from the Jesuit magazine *The Irish Monthly*; Yeats's friendship with Fr. Russell did not exempt him from a largely unfavourable review:

> The . . . mistaken notion of "representativeness" has, I think, spoiled almost the whole selection, in which the rollicking, savage, and droll elements are much too largely represented. We are far nicer people than the American or English reader will gather from these samples.[26]

Such criticism is familiar enough to anyone following the Irish reaction to *The Countess Cathleen* and the later productions of the Abbey Theatre, but it should be noted that Yeats was already encountering it ten years earlier in response to his edited work.

The specifically English reaction to *Representative Irish Tales* followed the same lines. The notice in *The Saturday Review* disallowed Yeats his title, suggesting that the tales were representative of 'that killing kind of humour which lives by stupid puns forced into the mouth of a stupider mannequin' and 'of their authors' peculiar styles.'[27] More revealing is the kind of story *The Saturday Review* singles out for limited praise. One of these is Rosa Mulholland's 'The Hungry Death', a melodramatic little story of famine on a Western island in which selfishness is shown to be only a transitory quality, while heroic sacrifice is more typical of the islanders. *The Saturday*

Review says of Miss Mulholland, 'she is almost the only one who gives us anything of the "Kindly Irish of the Irish"; the rest directed their best energies to forcing the stage business and gag of the screaming farcical kind . . .'. The review concludes with the hope 'that Mr. Balfour's light railway may bring the far-Western fish and the markets for it more closely acquainted.'[28] (The isolation of the island had made the famine particularly severe.)

In retrospect, the particular biases of the Irish and English reviewers are clear enough. While ostensibly condemning the stereotyped buffoonery of some of the pieces in *Representative Irish Tales* (a justifiable criticism to a point), their own presumptions about Irish fiction were equally questionable — that it should present a positive and idealized image of the Irishman to English and American readers, that the true nature of the Irish was pious and sentimental, and that the troubles of Ireland could not be tragic but simply the result of social and technological weaknesses capable of simple amelioration ('Mr. Balfour's light railway').

Yeats's response to these reviews was mild enough. In a letter to Katharine Tynan, he takes some satisfaction that *The Irish Monthly* had discovered 'the cloven hoof in my *Irish Tales*,' (presumably the 'rollicking, savage, and droll elements' the reviewer had faulted) (*Letters*, 174). He could also balance this against a favourable notice in *The Academy*, though this was by T. W. Rolleston, a fellow Celtophile, and for this reason a more predictable review.[29]

There was one failing gleefully pointed out by the *Irish Monthly* reviewer that Yeats could not easily dismiss. Yeats's single selection by William Maginn, 'Father Tom and the Pope', was a mistaken attribution. At its first appearance in *Blackwoods* in May, 1838, 'Father Tom and the Pope' was generally attributed to Maginn or John Fisher Murray, but by the time Yeats collected *Representative Irish Tales*, it was widely known (at least in Dublin) that Samuel Ferguson was the true author. This incident, small in itself, shows the result of Yeats's hasty reading and indicates a certain carelessness in his editing that was not necessarily to improve as he found more leisure for it.

The reviewer in *The Irish Monthly* had noted with approval that Yeats's version of 'Father Tom and the Pope' was bowdlerized, though he would have preferred it left out entirely.[30] Yeats had in fact cut Chapter IV of the story in which Father Tom, after much carousing and heated debate, had 'made free with the two lips ov Miss Eliza,' that is, had kissed the Pope's housekeeper to the scandal of 'his Riv'rence' and the reviewer.[31] Yeats undoubtedly felt that while Fr. Tom's drinking would be tolerated by his readers, indelicacies would not. He was willing to make an accommodation — to a point.

By 1892, an initial period in Yeats's editorial career was over. The subjects had been entirely Irish — two books of folk and fairy tales and two of fiction. Though it is difficult to imagine, Yeats's reputation at this point must have been equally that of poet and editor, with perhaps the balance dropping towards the latter, since he had published only two books of poetry by 1892, precocious though they were.

In a letter to *The Freeman's Journal* in September of 1892, Yeats claims (with some satisfaction) 'A somewhat considerable experience of the editing of cheap books — I have edited five, some of which were sold in thousands . . .'.[32] Though he had edited by himself only four books by this time (Yeats may have been counting *Poems and Ballads of Young Ireland* as the fifth), the exaggeration was probably not simple egotism but a tactic to prove himself the likely candidate to gain control of a whole series of books on Irish subjects. 'The New Irish Library' controversy is discussed later, but it is typical that Yeats's editions, while undeniably a vital source of income, were also inextricably bound to his programme for Irish literature. This scheme involved searching Ireland's proximate past for imaginative literature that was distinctively Irish, uncorrupted by the scepticism and scientism he perceived in England and by English stereotypes of Irishmen, but also a literature of respectable artistic merit. Through judicious editing, which at times extended to the actual rewriting of his material, Yeats was able to isolate such a literature and present it to the Irish reading public and his contemporary writers as a testimonial to a distinctively Irish imagination and a model for the future.

II

There is an unmistakable continuity between Yeats's first strictly poetic anthology, A Book of Irish Verse (1895), and the compilations of folklore and fiction that had preceded it since 1888. This continuity was, most importantly, a matter of intention and philosophy, but it extended also to the poets Yeats was interested in. For example, all the poets represented in Fairy and Folk Tales (except Yeats himself), Allingham, Ferguson, and Mangan, to name a few, appear again in A Book of Irish Verse, often with the same poems. Yeats's intention was again the reciprocal activity of discrimination and conservation. Just as he had rescued what he considered the best of Carleton from the oblivion of the second-hand book stalls, so also he snatched 'stray ballads and lyrics' from the uneven output of a large number of Irish poets to make A Book of Irish Verse (Letters, 250).

Because the movement to promote Irish literature was further advanced than at the publication of Fairy and Folk Tales, (in good part because of his own activities), Yeats had a clearer conception of the audience for A Book of Irish Verse. While he had hoped that Fairy and Folk Tales would be useful to emerging Irish poets of his own persuasion as a source of 'plots and atmosphere,' he now aimed at a larger but still select readership:

> This book differs also from some of its kind, in being intended only a little for English readers, and not at all for Irish peasants, but almost wholly for the small beginning of that educated and national public, which is our greatest need and perhaps our vainest hope.[33]

The fact that Yeats believed this emerging audience was being poorly served by Sir Charles Gavan Duffy's 'New Irish Library' certainly imparted a sense of urgency to his anthology.

Yeats, at about the time he was selecting Representative Irish Tales, got the idea of issuing an inexpensive series of books on Irish subjects that would serve to epitomize the new national movement and educate popular Irish taste at the same time. But Charles Gavan

Duffy (the originator of the first 'Irish Library' and an associate of 'Young Ireland') proposed the same idea independently of Yeats and at about the same time. While it looked for a while as if Yeats and Duffy could combine their schemes, it soon became evident that Duffy would be content to memorialize 'Young Ireland', a literary and nationalist movement that had flared briefly between 1842 and 1848, while Yeats held out for work of his own generation.[34] The alternatives, as Yeats saw them, were a return to the poetry of the Young Irelanders with its criteria of 'patriotism and political effect,' or the establishment of a new national poetry based on 'literary standards.'[35] While Yeats lost in his attempt to model the 'New Irish Library' after his own plan, his dispute with Duffy shaped his Introduction and the contents of *A Book of Irish Verse* no less than his stated principle that he chose according to what gave him pleasure.[36]

In the Introduction to the 1895 edition of *A Book of Irish Verse* (there was a revised edition in 1900), Yeats surveys over a hundred years of Irish poetry and establishes roughly five periods in the chronicle of Irish poetry to the 1890's. In the first were some 'faintly' Irish authors such as Swift, Goldsmith, and Sheridan — in Yeats's opinion (at least in 1895), Irishmen only by accident of geography or Irishmen who chose to treat 'English scenery and manners.'[37]

Thomas Moore was a transitional figure to the next group, the poets of Young Ireland with Thomas Davis at the centre and the figure of James Clarence Mangan at the periphery. Yeats gives Mangan special attention, but his judgment on the rest was uncompromising despite the continuing popularity of the Young Irelanders in 1895: 'in the main the poets who gathered about Thomas Davis, and whose work has come down to us in "The Spirit of the Nation," were of practical and political, not of literary importance.'[38]

The next group is of special significance because, in Yeats's mind, they proved that literary standards could survive in a period of intense nationalism. Ferguson, Allingham, and Aubrey De Vere are described, in the 1895 edition, as 'working quietly as men of letters,' a phrase that by the 1900 edition had become 'working apart from politics,' and the descriptions are in fact interchangeable in Yeats's phraseology.[39] Yeats on occasion described his own role as that of a 'man of letters,' and it seems clear that the 'Independents', Ferguson, Allingham, and De Vere, provided precedents for his own difficult role in the 1890's as mediator between poetry and politics.

After a deferential glance at the Fenian poets, Yeats turns to his contemporaries whom he considers the successors of the 'Independents'. In the 1895 edition these are Douglas Hyde, Lionel Johnson, Thomas Rolleston, and Katharine Tynan; by the time of the revised 1900 edition Yeats had made some reassessments and Miss Nora Hopper and Æ (George Russell) are added to the list while Hyde and Rolleston are dropped. As with Ferguson, Allingham, and De Vere, the governing quality of their poetry is its 'deliberate art' even though they are 'more anxious to influence and understand Irish thought' than their three predecessors.[40]

The inclusions in *A Book of Irish Verse* follow rather predictably from the judgments of Yeats's Introduction. Generally this means that the poets of Young Ireland, Davis, McGee, Doheny, and Walsh, are scantily represented with many of the movement omitted entirely, while Ferguson, Allingham, and De Vere and those poets Yeats considered their successors are amply included.

If one of the strong emphases of *A Book of Irish Verse* is poetic integrity over politics, another is the primacy of Irish material. Except in a very few instances, 'no Irishman living in Ireland has sung excellently of any but a theme from Irish experience, Irish history, or Irish tradition.'[41] While Yeats transforms this statement into an editorial principle, in his inclusions he is sometimes less than rigorous — as when he includes an excerpt from 'The Deserted Village' because of its tenuous connection with Irish history. (He had discovered that Goldsmith was drawing on memories of his native Lissoy in Ireland in the poem, though Yeats admits that 'the feeling and atmosphere of the poem are unmistakably English.'[42]) The principle of 'Irishness', as much as any other consideration, is responsible for the quality of *A Book of Irish Verse*.

Though the examples are few, there are some poems that Yeats has altered for *A Book of Irish Verse*, and these alterations are interesting because they are of the same kind that he has made in his collections of Irish fiction and folklore and thus show a continuity of editorial principle. The poets in question are, for the most part, quite minor figures, Gerald Griffin, Edward Walsh, and Alfred Perceval Graves.

Gerald Griffin's 'O'Brazil, The Isle of the Blest' describes 'A spectre island said to be sometimes visible on the verge of the western horizon, in the Atlantic, from the Isles of Arran.'[43] It is synonymous with Tir-na-nOg, a subject Yeats used frequently in early poems such as 'The White Birds' and 'The Man Who Dreamed of Faeryland'. Griffin's treatment in the first four stanzas is more allegorical than Yeats's, the simultaneous sense of attraction and danger, while alluded to, is not felt in the poem, and the concluding stanzas pervert Tir-na-nOg into a facile, strictly moral image. To salvage the poem, Yeats has cut the last two stanzas of 'O'Brazil, the Isle of the Blest' in both editions of *A Book of Irish Verse*:

> To you gentle friends, need I pause to reveal
> The lessons of prudence my verses conceal;
> How the phantom of pleasure, seen distant in youth,
> Oft lures a weak heart from the circle of truth.
> All lovely it seems like that shadowy Isle,
> And the eye of the wisest is caught by its smile;
> But, ah, for the heart it has tempted to stray
> From the sweet home of duty, away, far away![44]

Yeats has continued the process of refinement in other poems. In Edward Walsh's 'From the Cold Sod That's O'er You' he has removed the final sixth section, perhaps because it is merely bad, though the poem purports to be from the Irish, and it is difficult to tell whether the badness is from the original or the translation. In Alfred Perceval Graves's 'Father O'Flynn' Yeats has suppressed the dialect somewhat and minimized the refrain, perhaps in the first instance to soften the Irish stereotype. And Dora Sigerson's 'Can Doov Deelish' is unaccountably missing its third stanza in Yeats's version.

Even Yeats's contemporaries of the 1890's were not immune to his revisions, though the fact that living authors could complain as the dead could not, probably kept down the number of Yeats's more obvious revisions. There are two substantive changes in Lionel

Johnson's poem 'To Morfydd' that appear only in the *Book of Irish Verse* version, though they are minor in themselves.[45] On the other hand, the *Book of Irish Verse* version of Katharine Tynan's 'The Children of Lir' amounts to a more serious alteration.

Yeats alludes to the poem in a letter written in 1899 proposing a new edition of *A Book of Irish Verse* to Methuen and Co. (This letter incidentally shows Yeats very conscious of the momentum of the Irish literary movement and the importance of his own work to it.)

> I write to suggest that, as a larger and I think expensive anthology of Irish verse is coming out . . . under the editorship of Mr. Rolleston and with an introduction by Stopford Brooke, you return a number of the remaining copies of my anthology and reissue them with a new preface and a certain amount of new pages at the end. If you agree to reprint the last forty pages and add a few new pages to them, I could bring the work up to date. I think that the reviews would be certain to sell off a good many copies. Our movement is now in a much more developed state. The new edition of my poems with Unwins, though there is no change from the first edition except some not very important revisions is selling remarkably well. It has sold more copies in a month than the old edition sold in a year or more. I believe the same thing could happen with "A Book of I.V." The talk about Rolleston's anthology would help us especially as Rolleston's big book will be much more expensive.
>
> Should you not wish to reprint the last forty pages I would be content to leave the book as it is, if I can correct a rather bad mistake on page 210 where certain verses, part of a poem got dropped out through a mistake of my copyist. I could leave out something else to make room.[46]

The 'bad mistake' Yeats refers to is the omission of the final forty lines of Katharine Tynan's 'The Children of Lir' in the 1895 *Book of Irish Verse*. It is possible that there is more to this omission than the oversight of a copyist (mentioned again in the Preface to the 1900 edition).

Katharine Tynan's poem is a treatment of the Irish legend in which Aoife, stepmother of Lir's children, jealous of their father's love for them, turns them into swans, in which shape they must continue for 900 years. The version printed in the 1895 *Book of Irish Verse* is a description of the swans as tragic symbols of abandonment. It has its roots in the legend of 'The Children of Lir', but there is little emphasis on the legend itself. There are a number of elements in the omitted stanzas following this description that Yeats might have objected to. In the sixth stanza Katharine Tynan intrudes herself into the poem, speaking of 'my swans' and suggesting that the sorrow of the swans is a result of their human natures imprisoned in the swan's form, though the legend itself stresses purely physical hardship. Neither the intrusion of the author nor the new theme is developed adequately in the rest of the poem which is an unconvincing dialogue between the homesick Hugh, Conn, and Fiachra and their consoling sister Finnuola. It seems unlikely (though possible) that the copyist would have omitted the very lines which make 'The Children of Lir' a lesser poem; certainly Yeats was capable of such a revision. One might conjecture that Katharine Tynan had complained to Yeats of the truncated version of the poem in the 1895 edition, and that he had restored the lines reluctantly. To keep her selection in balance, he removed another of her poems, 'In Iona'.[47] While it is true that Yeats has devalued Katharine Tynan's type of poetry in the revised Introduction to the 1900 *Book of Irish Verse*, her allotment remains the same, over ten pages, almost twice as much as even Æ's expanded representation.

Since *A Book of Irish Verse* became a sourcebook for a number of later Irish anthologies (which may have been one of Yeats's intentions), some of the revisions made in that collection were, it seems, perpetuated for an audience larger than that of Yeats's edition. To mention one important anthology, the ten volume *Irish Literature* edited by Justin McCarthy in 1904 repeated Yeats's shortened versions of 'O'Brazil, The Isle of the Blest' and 'The Children of Lir' as well as the abbreviated version of Carleton's 'The Fate of Frank M'Kenna' which had appeared in *Fairy and Folk Tales*.[48] To be sure, these versions could be the result of independent editorial judgment, but it seems likely that Yeats's editions were consulted for the revised versions of these pieces.

With the revised edition of *A Book of Irish Verse* in 1900, Yeats's early career as editor was almost complete. Certainly there were some projects that were not realized. All that has survived of one such scheme that cost Yeats a great deal of grief in 1891 and 1892, the 'Irish Adventurers' ('those wretched "Irish Adventurers" ') for T. Fisher Unwin, is a great deal of correspondence and an article on eighteenth century 'Irish Rakes and Duellists' in *United Ireland*. Yeats's scheme for a 'Library of Ireland', though appropriated by Sir Charles Gavan Duffy's 'New Irish Library' in 1893, was not to disappear entirely. It resurfaced over ten years later in a somewhat different form — and over the colophon of Dun Emer, later the Cuala Press.

III

Most of Yeats's editing in the 1890's (and in the few years on either side of the decade) has an obvious Irish quality. Two apparent exceptions are his editions of Blake and Spenser, but Yeats insisted on treating even these poets from an Irish vantage.

At the same time that Yeats was editing Irish folklore and fiction, he was at work on an edition of the poetry of William Blake (with Edwin Ellis, a painter and friend of J. B. Yeats). The task was accomplished over four years, and in February of 1893 *The Works of William Blake* (the so-called Quaritch edition) was published in three volumes, followed in the same year by *The Poems of William Blake*, edited by Yeats alone.[49]

There is general agreement about the importance of the Yeats-Ellis *Blake*. It provided the fullest, though not most accurate text of Blake in the nineteenth century, most importantly printing *Vala* (*The Four Zoas*) for the first time. The Quaritch edition takes Blake with a new seriousness, emphasizing not the isolated attractions of his poetry but the coherence of his symbolism (Yeats's essay 'The Symbolic System' was especially important in this respect). Finally, the Yeats-Ellis edition encouraged later editors to build on its strengths — and remedy its weaknesses.[50] Yeats touched on some of the shortcomings of the edition and elaborated his precise contribution to it in a note inscribed in Lady Gregory's copy of *The Works of William Blake*:

The work gives me no particular pleasure, at least my part does not. It is substantially correct in its interpretations but it is full of misprints for which I am not responsible as I saw only a few of the proofs; and its descriptions of the doctrine of more ancient myths than Blake are inadequate, in one or two cases when I have tried to read Blake in this light I have blundered through not having enough light — as in the attributions of the tribes of Israel.
P.S. The book was written in this way. I wrote a life of Blake almost as long as my life of him in 'The Muses' Library Book', an account of the symbolic system as a whole and a short interpretive argument of each prophetic work. Ellis expanded, or rather completely rewrote the life into its present form, he accepted with some alteration and modification the chapters of the symbolic system, and expanded the short arguments to ten times their original length; and wrote a number of extra chapters. . . . His mind was far more minute than mine but less synthetic. I had a tendency to make generalizations on imperfect foundation, and he to remain content with detached discoveries. We worked almost four years and our method was to collate every mention of a mythological personage, or symbol. Ellis compiled a concordance to aid us.
With the exception of the part called "The Symbolic System" almost all of the actual writing is by Ellis.[51]

One failing that Yeats does not mention (though the critics do), is the inadequate text of the Quaritch Blake. With Blake, Yeats, for his part, confronted an editing problem of a magnitude he had not faced before, or would again. Blake's poems were largely unpublished at his death, and his manuscripts were chaotic at best (this is especially true of *Vala*). Blake's earlier editors (Swinburne and the Rossettis) redoubled the confusion by altering or 'improving' his texts, asserting or at least implying that they did this because Blake was careless, uneducated, or unstable. Yeats and Ellis took the practices of these earlier editors as a precedent rather than a warning, and they regularized metre, deleted, transposed, and substituted words and phrases in order to rescue Blake's poems 'from

3. Title page: *The Works of William Blake*,
Volume I of three volumes, London 1893. 10 × 6¼".

THE WORKS
OF
WILLIAM BLAKE

Poetic, Symbolic, and Critical

EDITED WITH LITHOGRAPHS OF THE ILLUSTRATED
"PROPHETIC BOOKS," AND A MEMOIR
AND INTERPRETATION

BY

EDWIN JOHN ELLIS
Author of "Fate in Arcadia," &c.

AND

WILLIAM BUTLER YEATS
Author of "The Wanderings of Oisin," "The Countess Kathleen," &c.

"Bring me to the test
And I the matter will re-word, which madness
Would gambol from"
Hamlet

IN THREE VOLS.

VOL. I

LONDON
BERNARD QUARITCH, 15 PICCADILLY
1893
[*All Rights Reserved*]

the wonderfully careless and self-confuting form in which they were left by the hasty hand that created, but would not control them.'[52] Yeats's own edition of Blake was little better in this respect. Despite his claim that he had 'simply reprinted Blake's own text,'[53] *The Poems of William Blake* contains some unique emendations while in other instances it follows the revisions of earlier editors.

The intention of Yeats's and Ellis's revisions must have seemed to them admirable — to give Blake to the world in his most impressive form even if this meant reworking his poems. Yeats at least had used the same rationale with his editions of Irish authors, though with writers like Carleton and Lover he concentrated on removing their 'impurities', whereas with Blake it was a matter of correcting his 'carelessness'.

Yeats was likely to see any subject from an Irish viewpoint in the 1890's and Blake was no exception. His most notorious attempt at Celtic assimilation is surely his claim in *The Works of William Blake* (repeated in his own edition) that Blake came from an Irish father. The claim rested on scant evidence and is generally discounted. Its significance for Yeats was that it made Blake, conveniently, a precursor of the enlightened Irishman, for Blake as an anti-materialist dissenter from English culture exemplified qualities Yeats generally took to be Irish. Yeats had less trouble locating Edmund Spenser physically in Ireland since he had lived there, not always happily, for twenty years, but in other ways he was harder to assimilate into Yeats's all-encompassing Celticism.

Yeats's edition of *Poems of Spenser* was published in 1906, but it is significant that Yeats made his selection and wrote his Introduction in 1902 (his publisher was apparently having difficulty with other books in the series and took four years to bring the Spenser out), for this is the Yeats of the 1890's more than of the decade following.

It is doubtful that Yeats would have edited *Poems of Spenser*, at least at this point in his life, if a publisher had not suggested it, but he approached the task with characteristic enthusiasm and originality. Nevertheless, he seems to have been disappointed by his intensive reading of Spenser in 1902, for Yeats's Introduction is a curious performance. He does not work up the reader's enthusiasm for his subject as is usual with such introductions. This is not altogether surprising for a critic who came to Spenser with an acquired dislike for allegory, but Yeats's dissatisfaction extends also to Spenser the man. Yeats saw Spenser as a seriously compromised poet, one of an earlier Tragic Generation than Lionel Johnson who was caught not between the Victorian and the Modern but between Merry England and the Puritans — in a conflict between 'esthetic and moral interests that was to run through well-nigh all his works . . .'.[54] According to Yeats, this made his allegory heavy-handed and unconvincing and distracted from his true interest, 'the beautiful and sensuous life he has called up before our eyes.'[55]

Yeats saw Spenser not only as an ambivalent esthete, but (more accurately) as a type of the Irishman by residence who nevertheless remains a stranger in Ireland. He had no feeling for the people or history of Ireland according to Yeats. Like other Englishmen in Ireland, (Thomas Parnell, from whose work Lennox Robinson selected a volume for the Cuala Press is another example,) he was a poet who could not recognize the native poetry of Ireland, a fantast blind to Ireland's 'kingdom of Faerie, of which his own poetry was often but an image in a broken mirror.'[56]

In his Introduction to *Poems of Spenser*, Yeats was explicit about his principle of selection: 'I have not tried to select what people call characteristic passages, for that is, I think, the way to make a dull book. One never really knows anybody's taste but one's own, and if one likes anything sincerely one may be certain that there are other people made out of the same earth to like it too.'[57] Yeats had declared himself 'bored by allegory', that most characteristic of Spenserian modes, considering it more wholly an intellectual construction than the product of 'wizard frenzy', and his selection from *The Faerie Queene* reflects this dislike. In Canto I, for example, he passes over the 'allegorical procession' of the Red Cross Knight and his company, choosing instead the Knight's encounter with Fraudibio who had been changed into a tree by Duessa, a scene that has a strange and fearsome atmosphere that would make it quite at home in Yeats's *Fairy and Folk Tales*. Elsewhere in his selection, in *The Shepheardes Calender* for example, Yeats, not unexpectedly, chooses on the whole the more idealized Arcadian segments (October, November, and December) over the more realistically rendered months.

Yeats's Spenser is by no means a scholarly edition. Its Introduction and selection are too eccentric for that, and its glossary and notes are only a half-hearted attempt. *Poems of Spenser* is a 'poet's edition', and in this kind of book an impressionistic introduction and an uncharacteristic selection might almost pass for a fresh view of a venerable subject, but it remains a hazardous edition for the student first coming to the poet.

IV

Yeats from 1899 to 1908 edited three 'occasional publications' dealing specifically with the Irish theatre, *Beltaine*, *Samhain*, and *The Arrow*.[58] They were sold originally with the theatre programmes of the Irish Literary Theatre (in its various forms). It should be said that Yeats was the editor of these theatre publications in a different, more partial way than for his *Fairy and Folk Tales* or *A Book of Irish Verse*, and this becomes increasingly true after the second number of *Samhain* (October, 1902) when it becomes almost a one-man publication.

The first number of *Beltaine* as originally published in May, 1899, does not specifically name Yeats as editor. In fact, in the section entitled 'Plans and Methods' where he corrects Lionel Johnson who had located *The Countess Cathleen* in the sixteenth century (insisting it was a symbolic rather than historical play), Yeats speaks of himself in the third person. This was not a serious attempt to disguise his direction of *Beltaine* (the anonymity was dropped with the second number), but it shows Yeats at some pains to give the theatre project at least the appearance of a broader base of support.

The first numbers of *Beltaine* and *Samhain* had contributions by not only Yeats but by his fellow founders of the Irish Literary Theatre, George Moore, Edward Martyn, and Lady Gregory as well as an article by C. H. Hereford (from the *Daily Express*) on 'The Scandinavian Dramatists', and approving press reviews of the first performances.[59] Altogether these suggest a more general support and approval for a project that was more Yeats's doing than he perhaps cared to admit at the time. It was important that the Irish Literary

Theatre did not appear to be the enterprise of one man but rather the culmination of a more universal national feeling.

Beltaine and the early *Samhain* present a fairly unified programme. Yeats, Moore, and Martyn, the three principal contributors, agree that the Irish theatrical experiment should not mimic the commercial theatre of England, that it should not be merely entertaining but should be 'literary' in the sense of demanding intellectual engagement. But there are differences of opinion that indicate the pluralism of the Irish Literary Theatre and its publications. Moore and Martyn

THREEPENCE—INCLUDING PROGRAMME.

BELTAINE

An Occasional Publication. Number One. May 1899.

THE ORGAN OF THE IRISH LITERARY THEATRE

LONDON: AT THE SIGN OF THE UNICORN.

DUBLIN: AT THE "DAILY EXPRESS" OFFICE.

4. *Beltaine*, No. 1, 1899. Front cover (reduced). Original 8½ × 6¾".

SAMHAIN

Edited for the Irish Literary Theatre by W. B. Yeats and containing a Play in Irish by Douglas Hyde with English translation by Lady Gregory and Articles by George Moore and by Edward Martyn. Published in October 1901 by Sealy Bryers & Walker in Dublin and by T. Fisher Unwin in London and sold at Sixpence.

5. *Samhain*, No. 1, 1901. Front cover (reduced). Original size 8¾ × 7″.

see the corruption of the English stage as a sign of the impending collapse of empire; Yeats attributes it to the effects of 'commercialism and materialism.'[60] He attempts, with accurate instinct, to turn the theatre from a simple reaction to English life to a celebration of peasant life and the heroic past of Ireland, preferably in poetic drama. Irish nationalism must not rest simply on hatred of England.

There is agreement in *Beltaine* and *Samhain* about the importance of Henrik Ibsen for the Irish Theatre, but some dispute as to why. Yeats's eventual position was that Ibsen should be consulted for his masterful construction; Moore and Martyn contended that his subject matter, 'the modern drama of society' was his proper bequest to the Irish theatre.[61] When Yeats joined with William Fay's company of Irish players (whose strength was peasant plays) Moore and Martyn severed themselves from the Irish Literary Theatre.

The second number of *Samhain* reflects this schism. With the departure of Moore and Martyn, Yeats had lost two of his most active contributors. It is true that Lady Gregory remained, but her pieces for *Beltaine* and *Samhain* had been of the order of programme notes; she was a practising dramatist rather than a theoretician. For the second number, Æ (George Russell) temporarily became spokesman for the theatre; in 'The Dramatic Treatment of Heroic Literature' he counters Standish O'Grady's assertion in the *All Ireland Review* that the ancient Irish heroic cycles were not suitable for dramatic presentation because they could only be sensationalized and degraded on the stage. (Æ's *Deirdre* had proved the contrary.) But a collaboration between Yeats and Æ in *Samhain* was ultimately impossible because Yeats distrusted Æ's democratic instincts, thinking that his influence would open the Irish theatre to inferior work.

The exodus of Yeats's collaborators and his own increasing confidence in his understanding of the theatre resulted in a *Samhain* that was almost entirely Yeats's own publication. It is true that he regularly printed there the current plays at the Abbey and occasional press notices, but the theoretical statements were entirely his. For this reason *Samhain* after 1902 is of less interest from the point of view of Yeats's editing, though not from other perspectives.

II DUN EMER AND THE CUALA PRESS

I

The Dun Emer Press began publishing in 1903 as part of a larger enterprise, the Dun Emer Industries, founded by an Irishwoman, Evelyn Gleeson, after the inspiration of William Morris's Arts and Crafts Movement. W. B. Yeats's sister, Elizabeth Yeats (Lolly), with various assistants, was directly responsible for the Press until her death in 1940. In 1908, because of internal disagreements, the Press severed its connections with the Industries (and Miss Gleeson) becoming the Cuala Press at a new location, Churchtown, not far from Dublin. There followed a good many more dislocations and reorganizations, but the Press had a remarkable intellectual continuity despite them. This can be attributed largely to W. B. Yeats who, from 1903 until his death in 1939 (with a brief interruption), served as its editorial advisor.

In general the volumes from Dun Emer and Cuala follow rather closely the rhythm of Yeats's hopes and frustrations. The first ten years of the Press coincide roughly with Yeats's intense involvement with the Irish Dramatic Movement. Following the hostile reaction to Synge's plays, there is a gradual withdrawal from the goal of a popular literature for Ireland. 'Unity of Culture', one of Yeats's most persistent ideals, becomes something found increasingly only in the past or in other cultures. Yeats loses touch with what is happening on a popular level in Ireland; there is some irony in the fact that one of the most esoteric volumes from Cuala (Pound's Noh plays) was published the same year as the Easter Rising (1916), but that event is commemorated only in a colophon. But the cycle reverses, and once again, towards the end of Yeats's life, Cuala is publishing translations from the Irish rather than the Japanese and Bengali as well as broadsheets of popular Irish songs and ballads.

What follows deals particularly with two authors who uniquely affected the direction of the Press, Æ (George Russell) and John M. Synge. Æ attempted direct intervention to make the Press conform to his own idea of what an Irish press should publish. Yeats's strong reaction set a rather conservative tone for what it actually did publish. In contrast Synge's influence was most indirect. He did not, as Æ had, concern himself with more than his own work published by Cuala, and he was dead by the time the Press was six years old, but his spirit, in the form of his own beliefs about poetry, troubled Yeats for decades.

Yeats believed in vigorous editing as his practice in the 1890's proves. Analyzing the demise of *The Shanachie*, a short-lived Dublin quarterly, Yeats attributed it to 'vagueness of mind' and asserted: 'I do not find in the editing of this magazine any one selective mind or any one principle of selection. . . . I don't believe it is possible to make a good magazine without making up your mind who it is for whom you are making it and keeping to that idea throughout' (*Letters*, 474). Yeats, if asked, would surely have extended his principle to book publishing, and one can ask his questions of Dun Emer and Cuala: What is the principle of selection and for whom was the series intended?

In the Introduction to Pound's selection, *Certain Noble Plays of Japan* (1916), Yeats felt compelled to explain the presence of a volume of Noh plays in a series which to that point had been almost exclusively Irish in character: 'In the series of books I edit for my sister I confine myself to those that have I believe some special value to Ireland, now or in the future. I have asked Mr. Pound for these beautiful plays because I think they will help me to explain a certain possibility of the Irish dramatic movement.'[62] The principle guiding Yeats in directing the Press is clear enough from this statement, though admittedly quite general. Some questions remain. For a book to have some 'special value to Ireland' must it be by an Irish author about an Irish subject? A strict reading of Yeats's statement would suggest not, but the list of publications from the Press by 1916 argues otherwise. It implies that Yeats generally required an Irish author and Irish subject matter for Dun Emer and Cuala. When one or both conditions are not met, he usually feels some explanation is in order. Lord Dunsany was an Irishman, but his fables were not very Irish in milieu, so Yeats provided a long introduction arguing that his use of imagination is peculiarly Irish. The selection of Noh plays required a special apology for it was neither by an Irishman nor on an Irish subject. In 1933 Yeats, writing to Olivia Shakespear, confirmed the principle of Irishness:

> I wish I could put the Swami's lectures into the Cuala series but I cannot. My sister's books are like an old family magazine. A few hundred people buy them all and expect a common theme. Only once did I put a book into the series that was not Irish — Ezra's Noh plays — and I had to write a long introduction to annex Japan to Ireland (*Letters*, 807).

Yeats apparently forgot another exception, Tagore's *The Post Office*, but he affirms the principle by acknowledging his occasional departure from it.

Yeats, in the Introduction to the Cuala *Selections from the Writings of Lord Dunsany* (1912), is more explicit about the audience he envisions for the limited editions of the Press. In contrast to Duffy's 'New Library of Ireland' (discussed in Part I), the Cuala editions were 'intended for few people' and were written with an 'elaborate beauty' that made no attempt to be comprehensible to the peasant, though this was one of the touchstones of the Young Ireland movement. Even if Yeats had not specified his audience for Dun Emer and Cuala, the style of the Press makes this clear enough, carefully-crafted, relatively expensive limited editions obviously intended for a select readership.[63] The format is in direct contrast to Duffy's publications. Where the 'Library of Ireland' had made available through cheap reprints the poetry of Young Ireland to a large group of Irish readers (a practice Duffy re-established in the 'New Irish Library'), Dun Emer and Cuala aimed at the same audience that Yeats had cultivated for *A Book of Irish Verse*, the Irish 'leisured classes' that did not seem to know that their country had a literature of its own.[64]

If one examines the eight volumes published by the Dun Emer Press from 1903 to 1907 (excluding Yeats's own work), the continuity with Yeats's preoccupations in *A Book of Irish Verse* is inescapable. The enthusiasms are very much the same, Æ, Douglas Hyde, John Eglinton, William Allingham, and Katharine Tynan. If a projected volume of selections from Samuel Ferguson and Aubrey De Vere had materialized, the list would have corresponded even more obviously with Yeats's poetic canon of *A Book of Irish Verse*.[65] The only new name in Dun Emer was Lady Gregory whom Yeats had not met until after the first publication of *A Book of Irish Verse* and whose work for the Irish Revival was yet to come.[66]

An obvious explanation for the strong retrospective quality of Dun Emer was that these books constituted unfinished business: these were writers Yeats was likely to have published in the 1890's in his own library scheme, but Duffy's 'New Irish Library' prevented this. Yet there was another factor.

Æ, Douglas Hyde, and Katharine Tynan were established literary figures by 1903, at least in the context of the Revival; in fact a new generation of Irish writers was already apparent. Their patron was not Yeats but Æ. Of these mostly younger poets whom Æ helped, the more familiar today are Padraic Colum, Seumas O'Sullivan, and James Stephens, though more names from a later generation could be added to the list. In 1904, a year after the first volumes from Dun Emer, Æ presented to Irish readers a selection of promising poets in *New Songs*.[67] The selection included, besides Colum and O'Sullivan, Eva Gore-Booth, Thomas Keohler, Alice Milligan, Susan Mitchell, George Roberts, and Ella Young. Perhaps to forestall a likely criticism, Æ in his Preface to *New Songs* asserts: 'There may be traces here and there of the influence of other Irish poets, but there is no mere echoing of greater voices . . .'.[68] A reading of the poems in *New Songs* determines that Æ is exactly wrong. To be sure, Colum's 'A Poor Scholar of the 'Forties' and 'The Plougher' show some power and originality. But most of the others give a distinct sense of the familiar. For example, George Roberts's 'The Call' is a very close imitation of Yeats's 'The Lake Isle of Innisfree'. In other moods, Roberts can imitate Æ as in 'Earth and the Infinite', while Ella Young and Susan Mitchell mine the same devotional themes already so familiar from Katharine Tynan's work.

In many respects then, *New Songs* is a dimmer version of the group of Irish poets of 'The Celtic Twilight' mood Yeats had collected in *A Book of Irish Verse*. Unsurprisingly, Yeats found little to praise in *New Songs*. In a letter to Æ, he complained that a number of poems in the anthology not only imitated his own poetry but a mood in his work he found unsatisfactory because of its 'exaggeration of sentiment and sentimental beauty' (*Letters*, 434). He suggests too that his young imitators had arbitrarily fastened on this kind of poetry without the necessary personal involvement.

While it may be unreasonable to suggest that *New Songs* by itself accounts for the somewhat conservative character of the titles from Dun Emer (in respect of the publication of new work), Æ's anthology was certainly a factor. It was not only that Yeats was perhaps reluctant to trespass on Æ's literary domain; he also doubted that the poets about Æ ('Russell's poultry yard' as he called them) were pointing the direction to Ireland's imaginative future, one of his requirements for publication by the Press. Later in the history of Cuala Yeats was to admit some younger poets, (Frank O'Connor and F. R. Higgins are notable examples,) but these poets became Yeats's own proteges though not his imitators.

To this point the discussion has centred on Æ's oblique influence on Dun Emer. But he also tried to determine the course of the Press more directly. In September 1904 the Dun Emer Press was going through one of its periodic financial crises. It was at this point that the Dun Emer Industries Limited was formed to put the company on a better financial basis.[69] As part of the reorganization an advisory committee was formed and Æ was appointed a member; it must have been from this position that he attempted to 'democratize' the Press, presumably by lobbying for the inclusion of his poets from *New Songs*. A letter Yeats wrote to Katharine Tynan in September 1906 indicates that Æ's influence was felt for some time at Dun Emer:

> He [Æ] gets support from everyone who dislikes discipline, and from others that like him but do not understand the issue. He very nearly wrecked our theatre, and it is he who has influenced my sisters at this moment. When Starkie seceded from the Theatre where his acting was worse than his poetry he brought out with him a charming young woman who embroiders for my sisters [Maire Nic Shiubhlaigh (Maire Walker)], and this has kept them more or less in the midst of the discussions. It is all really one dispute. I have no doubt my sisters will learn before very long that I am right about the books as they have learned that I was right about the theatre. The trouble is that Russell in himself is perfectly charming because he suffers fools

gladly. His very mischief is a logical expression of his genius. The idea that my sisters should permit me to exclude good worthy people from their series of books merely because they write badly fills his soul with sorrow. He even pressed upon us the production of a play the hero of which was a giant eight feet high, rather than hurt the feelings of a friend.[70]

Æ's egalitarianism was not successful at Dun Emer, and one result was that he alienated Yeats, and in fact their friendship lapsed for almost ten years.[71] This episode very likely also confirmed Yeats's determination to publish only proven work at the Press.

II

With the works of John M. Synge, the newly reorganized Cuala Press took on a different character, more contemporary, looking less to the past. Yeats had found a young writer he could enthusiastically promote. But with Synge's work Yeats's involvement with the Press became (at least for a period) even more intense and a source of worry about more than that perennial problem, finances. In the period of Dun Emer many of Yeats's efforts had been of the diplomatic kind, as for example a request to Mrs. Allingham to reprint some of her husband's poems. Certainly there had been disagreements with Æ and John Eglinton, but these did not progress much beyond a small group. The trouble over Synge became a more public matter of contracts and estates.

Two Synge first editions appeared from Cuala within sixteen months of his death from cancer in March, 1909: *Poems and Translations* and *Deirdre of the Sorrows*. Synge's life and work were to provide something of a centre for Cuala in the next twenty years with John Masefield's *John M. Synge: A Few Personal Recollections* (1915), Yeats's *Synge and the Ireland of His Time* (1911), and *The Death of Synge* (1928), excerpts from a journal Yeats began in 1909 (and later incorporated in his *Autobiographies*).

Yeats's contribution to Synge's *Poems and Translations* was not strictly speaking editorial, since Synge was himself responsible for the selection and saw the book through the proof stage some two months before his death.[72] But Yeats did exercise one editorial function in acquiring *Poems and Translations* for Cuala, and the negotiations were complex and not altogether clear even now. Synge had apparently offered the poems first to the Dublin publisher George Roberts of Maunsel and Co. If Roberts was interested Synge had resolved to get Yeats's opinion on their quality before proceeding. Roberts was very definitely interested, but because Yeats had been involved with the publication of Synge's earlier work, he agreed that Yeats should be given a chance to judge the poems. According to Roberts, Yeats was not, though, to have a veto in the matter; Synge told him that he might publish the poems even if Yeats disliked them.[73]

Yeats had before this point apparently seen only some of Synge's early poems, and he was afraid they would only injure his reputation if published.[74] Seeing Synge's latest work, Yeats changed his mind and began talking of publication with Dun Emer (soon to be the Cuala Press). What Yeats probably proposed to Synge was the same plan so often adopted before at Dun Emer, a limited edition of the poems from his sister's press followed by a trade edition, in this case at Roberts's publishing house. Yeats might also have promised a speedy publication (Elizabeth Yeats's letters to Synge suggest this understanding), and this may have been persuasive to the ailing Synge; he might after all see the poems in print before he died. In any case, on 1 October 1908, he gave Yeats the manuscript of his poems, on 5 October he signed a contract with George Roberts for the trade edition, and the next day sailed for Coblence via London for a health cure.

Though Roberts had agreed to this arrangement, he was none too happy about Yeats's intervention. The Cuala edition probably prevented a separate Maunsel publication (at least immediately), for Synge's poems could not be expected to sell as well as his plays, the distinction between a limited and a trade edition being rather meaningless in this instance. In fact, Synge's poems first appeared from Maunsel as part of a collected edition in 1910.

The Cuala publication of *Poems and Translations* casts doubt on Yeats's business practices in this instance. As some slight defence of Yeats, Synge does not seem to have known his own mind, and he apparently treated his understanding with Roberts rather casually himself. Yeats's original Preface to Synge's *Poems and Translations* quotes a letter from Synge telling of Roberts's interest in his poetry, but the whole matter has been removed from the version of the Preface in Yeats's *Essays and Introductions*. It seems Yeats thought the whole episode best forgotten, for whatever reason.

Synge's Preface to *Poems and Translations* had an importance for Cuala all out of proportion to its brief length, for it began a dialogue in Yeats's mind about what kind of work the Press should publish. Yeats's prefaces and introductions to some ensuing volumes from Cuala can be taken as Yeats's continuing response to Synge's 'manifesto'. Synge had written in part:

> The poetry of exaltation will be always the highest, but when men lose their poetic feeling for ordinary life, and cannot write poetry of ordinary things, their exalted poetry is likely to lose its strength of exaltation, in the way men cease to build beautiful churches when they have lost happiness in building shops. . . . Even if we grant that exalted poetry can be kept successful by itself, the strong things of life are needed in poetry also, to show that what is exalted, or tender, is not made by feeble blood.[75]

Three years after *Poems and Translations*, in 1912, Yeats made *Selections from the Writings of Lord Dunsany* for Cuala. Primarily a writer of fantasy, Dunsany set his plays and stories in mythical regions like 'Babbulkund' and the basin of the 'River Yann', places far removed from Synge's Wicklow and Kerry. Yeats's long Introduction is in part an apology to the partisans of Young Ireland for Dunsany's non-Irish fantasy, in part a reply to Synge's Preface to *Poems and Translations*. In his Introduction Yeats appropriates Dunsany as one of 'the writers of our school' and contrasts him with the poets and novelists of Young Ireland. The latter had written to be generally understood and according to an 'ideal of reliable invariable men and women'. Yeats considered his own school 'unpopular', presenting an ideal of 'elaborate beauty' to a relative few. While the emerald green covers of the books from Young Ireland had symbolized an aggressive and superficial nationalism, the volumes from Dun

SELECTIONS FROM THE WRITINGS
OF LORD DUNSANY

THE CUALA PRESS
CHURCHTOWN
DUNDRUM
MCMXII

6. Title page of *Selections from the Writings of Lord Dunsany*, 1912.

Emer and Cuala, it is suggested, would survive a narrow nationalism and would constitute a literary past for future students, perhaps one more useful than Yeats himself had encountered in the old 'Library of Ireland'.

Lord Dunsany, according to Yeats, had in his fables created 'subtle elaborate emotions' through an imagined world; the suggestion is that this compensated for the absence of a strictly Irish milieu in his work. Dunsany's 'Babbulkund', from this point of view, is another 'Land of Heart's Desire', and for this reason he writes in one of the traditions of the Irish Revival, along with Æ and at least the early Yeats. But there was another more realistic strain in the history of the Revival too. Synge had seen the world as 'a withered and witless place' in comparison with Dunsany's fables. Yeats's Introduction, in defending Dunsany's use of imagination, can be read as a rejoinder to Synge's call for a literature of 'ordinary life'. Yeats asserted of Dunsany:

> His work which seems today so much on the outside, as it were, of life and daily interest, may yet seem to those students I have imagined rooted in both. Did not the Maeterlinck of "Pelleas and Melisande" seem to be outside life? and now he has so influenced other writers, he has been so much written about, he has been associated with so much celebrated music, he has been talked about by so many charming ladies, that he is less a vapour than that Dumas *fils* who wrote of such a living Paris.[76]

It is a credit to the endurance of Synge's thought that Yeats was still responding to it three years after the dramatist's death. Yeats for his part was obviously trying to maintain some choices for Irish writing, fearing that a strong demand for realism might stifle more exotic growth, as for example his own plays for dancers a few years later.

With *Certain Noble Plays of Japan, Chosen and Finished by Ezra Pound* (1916), Yeats took Cuala even further away from Synge's kind of art. In his Introduction to *Certain Noble Plays* Yeats faced immediately the obvious problem of Japanese plays in an Irish series. 'I have asked Mr. Pound for these beautiful plays because I think they will help me to explain a certain possibility of the Irish dramatic movement.'[77] This possibility was an aristocratic dramatic form; scenery would be simplified, movement formalized and almost static, facial expression rendered irrelevant by masks. Character development would be relatively unimportant. The emphasis was not to be on theatrical business or even the speaking voice but on the words of the drama. Remembering and perhaps regretting the years spent at the Abbey, and his curse 'on plays / That have to be set up in fifty ways', he expected the new drama to have the advantage 'that it need absorb no one's life, that its few properties can be packed up in a box, or hung upon the walls where they will be fine ornaments.'[78]

To an extent Yeats's Introduction continues the dialectic begun with Synge in the Preface to *Poems and Translations* and elaborated in the Introduction to *Selections from the Writings of Lord Dunsany*. In an indirect response to Synge's call for a 'poetry of ordinary things', Yeats had suggested that the fantasies of Dunsany, seemingly so out of touch with 'ordinary life', might prove most relevant to it after all. The Noh plays and Yeats's equivalents were much closer to Dunsany's aristocratic fantasy than to the Rabelaisian element in Synge's poetry and plays. Like the traveller in Dunsany's 'The Fall of Babbulkund' or the priest and lovers in the Noh *Nishikigi*, the three musicians of Yeats's *At the Hawk's Well* inhabit 'some country of our dreams' quite removed from Synge's imaginative world.

Yeats ends his Introduction as he had begun it, pondering the question of relevance. If the Noh plays originate in a 'country of dreams' how could they speak to an Irish audience increasingly obsessed with realism? Yeats advances a tentative solution, 'yet it pleases me to think that I am working for my own country. Perhaps some day a play in the form I am adapting for European purposes may excite once more whether in Gaelic or in English under the slope of Slieve-na-mon or Croagh Patrick, ancient memories . . .'.[79] Yeats realized this hope was 'a fancy'. Probably with the memory of his own efforts at the Abbey for over ten years, he concludes that his best hope is the example of his own achievement — if that is convincing, he need not worry about being 'influential', 'for my writings if they be seaworthy will put to sea, and I cannot tell where they may be carried by the wind. Are not the faery-stories of Oscar Wilde, which were written for Mr. Ricketts and Mr. Shannon and for a few ladies, very popular in Arabia?'[80]

It is not suggested that Yeats's Introduction to these Japanese plays equates Synge and realism as a common force to be resisted. Synge is not in fact mentioned by name; nor were his plays fundamentally realistic. Nonetheless, Synge's theory and the popular taste of the Irish audience resisted Yeats's aristocratic experiments, though for different reasons, the first from the conviction that the drama must offer sustenance for the imagination after the analogy of a daily meal rather than an exotic banquet, and the second because the usual audience lacked the 'rich memory' for the allusion and innovation of a difficult form.[81]

III

After *Certain Noble Plays*, there is a change of direction in the books Yeats edited for Cuala, a protracted return to the 'poetry of ordinary things', not to peasant plays but to the literature of an earlier Gaelic Ireland through translations such as Robin Flower's *Love's Bitter Sweet* (1925) but more especially Frank O'Connor's *The Wild Bird's Nest* (1932) and *Lords and Commons* (1938). (Some of the original poetry in F. R. Higgins's *Arable Holdings* (1933) belongs here too.)

The translations by Flower and O'Connor were not the first from the Gaelic at Dun Emer and Cuala, though earlier translators such as Lady Gregory and Douglas Hyde had drawn mainly on the epic cycles of the seventh century and the folk poetry of the nineteenth. These new translations explored for the most part the intervening period; the emphasis tends to be on the professional Gaelic poet rather than the inspired amateur and the lyric and lament rather than the epic; thus the claims that have been made for their influence on the later Yeats. They were made possible by the increasing availability of the Irish texts through such publications as Thomas F. O'Rahilly's *Dánta Grádha* (1916).

Frank O'Connor, as a young writer, had attacked Yeats's poetry because, he contended, Yeats wrote 'neither in an Irish tradition nor for an Irish public.'[82] Eventually O'Connor relented because, he says, 'in the few years I had known him I had seen his [Yeats's] poetry getting nearer and nearer to my own ideal of poetry.'[83] For O'Connor this ideal was founded on a tradition running from Gaelic poetry through Mangan to Synge. After Synge, he could find few practitioners of poetry in a 'manly way — Synge's way', though he obviously hoped that the later Yeats would continue the tradition.

The mention of Synge in connection with poetry in Irish clarifies O'Connor's standard, for though Synge's poems were in English, and he seems not to have known early Irish lyrical poetry (*his* translations were from Ronsard and Petrarch), his original verse has the energy, the strangeness, and at times the coarseness of a poem such as the Irish 'Prayer for the Speedy End of Three Great Misfortunes' translated in O'Connor's *The Wild Bird's Nest*:

> There be three things seeking my death,
>   All at my heels run wild —
> Hang them, oh God, all three! —
>   Devil, maggot and child.[84]

Synge would have called the qualities of this poem 'the strong things of life' and he would have recognized 'Prayer' as in the same vein with his poem 'The Curse' or his ballad 'Danny'.

IV

At about the same time that Yeats was attracted to the poetry of an older Gaelic Ireland, he renewed his interest in a non-native form, the ballad. With the collaboration of F. R. Higgins and Dorothy Wellesley, he edited two series of traditional and modern ballads, *A Broadside*, for the Cuala Press in 1935 and 1937. In December of those years the monthly numbers were issued in bound volumes (each with an introduction) as *Broadsides*. The idea for this series originated in an earlier Cuala enterprise, Jack Yeats's *A Broadside* issued monthly from June 1908 to May 1915. This earlier series suggested too the manner of W. B. Yeats's 1935 revival, the alternation of traditional and modern ballads; for his modern examples

Jack Yeats published poems by Masefield, James Stephens, Ernest Rhys, Padraic Colum, as well as his own work. In the 'New Series' of *A Broadside* W. B. Yeats used some of these same authors and, in a further debt to Cuala, drew freely from the list of Cuala writers published just before *Broadsides*, notably for the work of F. R. Higgins, Oliver Gogarty, and Frank O'Connor.

The later series of *Broadsides* have a special importance in the Cuala series because they flank *The Oxford Book of Modern Verse* edited by Yeats and published in 1936. The first numbers were appearing monthly while Yeats was reading for that anthology, and the kind of poetry represented in *Broadsides*, 1935, was clearly reflected in the selection he made for the Clarendon Press. The reaction to the anthology sharpened Yeats's feeling that poetry should be more public; one way to accomplish this was to re-establish it as musical in a carefully defined sense. The result was both the *Broadsides* of 1937 with its introductory discussion of poetry and music and the poetry readings broadcast by Yeats from the BBC the same year.

Yeats's interest in the ballad in 1935 was of course a return to a much earlier preoccupation. Most of the poems in *Fairy and Folk Tales* were ballads or ballad adaptations, and there was a section of anonymous verse, mostly ballads, in *A Book of Irish Verse*. But as we have seen in Yeats's prefaces and introductions to Cuala, his interests for a time turned more exotic. For this and other reasons Yeats largely neglected the ballad for the first decades of the Cuala Press. It was during this period that *A Broadside*, 'First Series', was being issued from the Press, and Yeats's disinterest in the ballad explains, at least partially, why he had little involvement with this project, though he of course watched the other publications from the Press carefully. There is no simple explanation for Yeats's return to the ballad after 1930, but some critics see Yeats's severe illnesses from 1927 to 1929 as crucial: with a return to health came a new sense of the body's importance.[85] The vitality and spontaneity of the ballad must have appealed to Yeats in this mood. There were other reasons as well.

In his broadcast 'Modern Poetry' Yeats says that he wrote in the ballad form as a young man because it was an antidote to

'Victorian rhetorical moral fervour', since 'an old ballad is never rhetorical.'[86] By 1930 British poetry had been purged of a specifically Victorian rhetoric, but there was another kind of moral fervour, political, which Yeats thought detrimental to good poetry. Then too, he found in English poetry (especially Eliot's early work) realistic subject matter matched to 'rhythmical flatness', and he liked neither. The bold themes and the rhythmical animation of the ballad could, Yeats thought, prove a corrective to these qualities. But Yeats needed the help of other poets in reviving the ballad.

At seventy Yeats could not expect to write poetry, direct the Cuala Press, advise the Abbey, and edit his own and others' work, at least to the extent he had in the past. Also, Mrs. Yeats, it seems, was sceptical of the *Broadsides* enterprise, feeling that it was a diffusion of Yeats's talent.[87] For these reasons collaboration seemed a sensible compromise, and F. R. Higgins was a likely choice for the first series. He was an experienced editor, not only of trade journals but of literary magazines such as *Shamrock*, *Welfare*, and *To-morrow*. He was also something of a folk musician which Yeats was not, at times writing his poems to Irish tunes,[88] and Yeats was determined that the *Broadsides* should have musical settings. Higgins's poetry too was of the right kind for *Broadsides*, emphasizing folk themes and saturated with the diction of the peasant and the atmosphere of the West of Ireland. At least from the publication of Higgins's *The Dark Breed* (1924), ballads and ballad adaptations got equal representation with the folk lyrics more typical of his early work. Higgins eventually became Yeats's arbiter of what was the true folk tradition and what could be allowed in the ballad.[89]

There might be some irony in a series of carefully printed and illustrated broadsheets that were more likely to find their way into private collections than into the streets, but it was Yeats's intention in the *Broadsides* to re-establish old ballads and introduce new ones into popular currency. In his essay 'What is Popular Poetry' (1901) Yeats had realized that this kind of poetry did not spring spontaneously from the people at all, but came from identifiable poets. Often it was shallow poetry, but Yeats learned in time that it did not have to be. If poetry were written accessibly and with a bold rhythm, it might originate with an individual poet, but it could enter into the 'popular mind'. Yeats always had some examples to show that this had happened, that even his own poetry had been sung in the streets as if it were anonymous folksong.

Yeats in the *Broadsides* did not follow the proven route to popularity. In the Foreword to the 1935 series, he gives very little emphasis to political ballads, though he does admire their immediacy and force. The ballads and songs of the poets of *The Nation* had been published (with music) in *The Spirit of the Nation* almost a hundred years before, and Yeats had included a selection of their work in *A Book of Irish Verse*. But Yeats omitted these poets from *Broadsides* because their ballads were not authentic enough. For the same reason he also excluded the songs of Tom Moore from the series, though Moore in the popular mind was the most admired of Irish song writers. Yeats thought Moore had not the 'poet's rhythm' — his 'hurdy-gurdy rhyme' brought him 'half way to the music hall'. 'Neither his songs nor those of "Young Ireland", nor any songs set by professional musicians, have become folk-lore', 'he is confined to the schoolroom, the concert platform; ears trained by country singers reject him'.[90]

Yeats and Higgins had repudiated some of the proven sources for songs and ballads; one still available to them was traditional Irish broadsides. These were generally crude and poorly printed, and the subjects were often grotesque, bawdy, or naively patriotic. But these were not fundamental defects and in fact the *Broadsides* often capitalize on some of these qualities. The serious flaw in Anglo-Irish broadsides, Yeats admitted, was one of diction, an insensitivity to language. Gaelic balladeers of the eighteenth century (often country schoolmasters) had often only a mechanical understanding of English and a weakness for Latinate words. With perhaps Tagore in mind, Yeats compares them to 'Europeanised Indians'; they had 'perhaps fluent English yet understand nothing of the words but their dictionary meaning.'[91] The result was pedantry, a quality that permeates Anglo-Irish ballads. Though Yeats insisted on the traditional ballad formula, he knew that formulaic language detracted from the appeal of this kind of poetry and his own case for the ballad. Yeats's solution, as it had been for Tagore's devitalised language, was judicious editing.

In 1937, while contemplating an anthology for Macmillan on the order of *Broadsides* (it was never published), Yeats wrote Edith Shakleton Heald explaining his method: 'As in the case of the *Broadsides* many of the traditional songs will be worked over by Higgins and myself. You can imagine what an improvement it is when all "steeds" become "horses" and all "maids" "girls" ' (*Letters*, 894). Surprisingly, such simple changes do help. The Colleen Rue in the traditional ballad of that title protests to her flattering admirer: 'I am not Aurora, or the beauteous Flora, but a rural maiden to all men's view.' In the *Broadsides* version (November 1935) the Colleen declares herself not a 'rural maiden' but a 'rural female' and the ballad becomes, at least momentarily, alive and convincing. Since traditional Irish ballads often survive in multiple versions, it is not always easy to determine Yeats's and Higgins's revisions, but some other poems that seem to show their work are 'The Lowlands of Holland', 'The Song of the Ghost', and 'The Boyne Water'. In these the reworking is primarily structural, the splicing together of multiple versions to get the most satisfactory rendition of a poem. While many of the revisions are minor in themselves, cumulatively they represent an attempt on the part of Yeats and Higgins to make the Irish ballad in English more vital and uncorrupted than it actually was. In a way this was what Yeats had done for the Irish folk tale almost fifty years before. Then it was a matter of detaching the central tale from a sceptical context, here of refurbishing language, but the end result was not so very different.

Not all the revisions in the 1935 *Broadsides* are limited to traditional ballads. Yeats revised Higgins's 'The Ballad of O'Bruadir' for the November 1935 *Broadsides* and used a shorter version for *The Oxford Book of Modern Verse* the next year. Yeats's revisions begin with some minor changes in the second stanza (the first in the *Oxford Book*) but become more interesting in the fourth. They are made largely to clarify the narrative. (O'Bruadir is a pirate-rogue who is lured into friendship with a stranger, betrayed, and hanged. The ballad is narrated by one of his men in Higgins's poem.) Higgins wrote in the first version in *The Dark Breed*:

> He gripped hands with a stranger, who
>   said I'd rather grip
> O'Bruadir in glory on the water
> 'Well I'm your man,' said Bruadir
>   and you're aboard my ship
>   Rolling glory on the water.'

Yeats revises this to

> 'There's no man' said a stranger, 'whose
>   hand I'd sooner grip
>   Rolling glory on the water . . .' [92]

emphasizing the conversational and keeping the refrain regular ('Rolling glory on the water') until the last stanza when, as often in his own ballads, it turns functional and becomes an essential part of the narrative: 'We found O'Bruadir dangling within an airy tree, / Ghosting glory from the water!' Some time after this ballad appeared in *Broadsides*, Yeats wrote to Dorothy Wellesley (who had also been rewritten by Yeats): 'I learned from Higgins and now he learns from me, for he says I have and he has not the right diction.' [93] In the case of 'The Ballad of O'Bruadir' anyway, Yeats's lesson had taken a most direct form.

For the 1937 *Broadsides* Yeats wanted a new scheme. His work on *The Oxford Book of Modern Verse* the year before led him to extend the series to English authors. Instead of an alternation of old and new Irish ballads, he would print Irish and English poems side by side to show the larger possibilities of putting words to music. The *Oxford Book* gave him not only his authors but an English editor as well, Dorothy Wellesley, the Duchess of Wellington.

Yeats became interested in Dorothy Wellesley's poetry while reading for the *Oxford Book* and a correspondence and a friendship followed. He not only included a large selection of her poetry in the Oxford anthology but edited *Selections from the Poetry of Dorothy Wellesley* published the same year. The fact that Dorothy Wellesley was not only a poet but also an editor must have recommended her to Yeats for *Broadsides*. She had been the general editor of the 'Hogarth Living Poets', a series that published her work, that of her friend Virginia Sackville-West, the poetry of C. Day Lewis and the anthology *New Signatures* which introduced the young poets W. H. Auden, Julian Bell, Stephen Spender and others (this was specifically edited by Michael Roberts). Although the Hogarth series gave her attachments to Bloomsbury, Dorothy Wellesley never felt entirely comfortable with Virginia Woolf and her friends,[94] and this freedom from literary allegiances must have helped her friendship with Yeats. Like Yeats, Dorothy Wellesley never went to the university and was largely educated at home.[95] Unlike Yeats's, her home (by her own admission) was a 'Philistine environment'.[96] Her politics were compatible with Yeats's (except on Irish matters; she never liked his ballad on Roger Casement) and her poetry treats some of the same themes as Yeats's, the fading of the aristocracy in her poem 'Going, Going, Gone' for example.

Unsurprisingly, Yeats overwhelmed Dorothy Wellesley and her poetry. He seemed compelled to revise her work and many of the poems in her *Selections* show Yeats's hand.[97] Their painful correspondence over Dorothy Wellesley's ballad 'The Lady, The Squire, and the Serving-maid' shows the practice continuing into the *Broadsides* of 1937.[98] As co-editor of this series, Dorothy Wellesley did make some contributions, but most of the initiative came from Yeats, and she had enough humility to play the discrete partner, though when it came to Yeats trespassing on her poetry she could be stubborn.

Typically, both Yeats and Wellesley signed the Foreword to the 1937 *Broadsides* but the author was obviously Yeats, and he continued the theme from the earlier series, the right relation of words and music. Yeats wanted music because it would give his ballads wider currency and because with it he thought a modern diction could be admitted into poetry, though he was vague about how this could be done.[99] But in any case he did not want music obscuring the words of poetry. This emphasis on the words caused some consternation among his more musically-accomplished collaborators. V. C. Clinton-Baddeley was one of these, and he finally realized that Yeats did not want 'Words for Music' but 'Music for Words', music was to be strictly subordinate.[100] Despite his confusions about poetry and music, Yeats's larger concern seems clear. He wanted intelligibility and this same requirement led him to promote the traditional form of the ballad and to disparage what he saw as the shapelessness of Pound's *Cantos*. Specifically, the intelligibility he required was non-abstract, non-mathematical. He seemed to mistrust music as part of the 'flux', the formlessness impinging on the mind that he repudiated in the Introduction to the *Oxford Book*. As he wrote in the Foreword to the 1937 *Broadsides*, 'Music that wants of us [poets] nothing but images that suggest sound, cannot be our music.' He did not seem to understand that music could have its own kind of intelligibility, or if he did, how it could work in consort with that of poetry.

Not all the poems in the 1937 *Broadsides* were ballads and this marks a departure from the earlier series where all but a few of the twenty-four poems were ballads. Yeats undoubtedly felt constricted by one form, and the work in the 1937 series is both ballads and lyrics. Dorothy Wellesley recognized the change when she puzzled over Yeats's inclusion of Turner's 'Men Fade Like Rocks'; writing of this and other of Turner's poems she asked Yeats, 'Are they the right sort of things for *Broadsides*? I think *Broadsides* should be vigorous, tragic, bawdy, wild, any of those things. Am I right? But not contemplative.'[101] Yeats replied that Turner's poem was one of a number he planned to 'reflect the modern mind where most subtle',[102] and he obviously was prepared to expand the scope of the series to find new songs for music. (The 1937 *Broadsides* also contains poems by Higgins and James Stephens that are not ballads.) The juxtaposition of the lyric with a more robust strain is matched in the illustrations, Jack Yeats's for 'Come Gather Round Me, Parnellites' compared to Victor Brown's more elegant design for Dorothy Wellesley's 'Lass, Is Your Heart Dead?'.

Dorothy Wellesley and Yeats were to have collaborated on another set of *Broadsides* for 1939 but Yeats's death prevented it. Interestingly, the plans were to include some poets whom Yeats had slighted in the *Oxford Book*. An Auden poem was considered for the 1937 series, but it was never published. (Perhaps Auden refused his permission after he saw, or thought about, his selection in the *Oxford Book*.) For the 1939 series a poem by Auden was actually chosen as well as one by C. Day Lewis. Auden's selection was to be Number XXIV from *Look, Stranger!* beginning 'O for doors to be open and an invite with gilded edges', a ballad-like poem with a Yeatsian refrain, 'Cried the cripples to the silent statue, / The six beggared cripples'.[103] As different as 'O for doors to be open' is from Yeats's 'Beggar to Beggar Cried', Yeats seems to have found, belatedly, that one at least of the 'Ezra, Auden, Eliot school' had a common interest in ballads and song forms. But this was in 1938. A few years earlier, at the publication of *The Oxford Book of Modern Verse*, Yeats saw only their differences.

* * *

Yeats's editorial direction of Dun Emer and Cuala lasted for over thirty-five years. Obviously in such a long period there were influences at work other than those of Æ and John Synge, more enthusiasms than for the Noh play and the ballad. In a long Press list, there are just enough exceptions, enough volumes that stubbornly refuse to fall in place, to warn the critic against rationalizing the series too much, reminding him that the Press had its practical and fortuitous side too. Certainly the three volumes of poetry by Oliver Gogarty, classical in manner but with an underlying lyricism, stand somewhat apart and testify to the impact on Yeats of Gogarty's impetuous personality. Lady Gregory's *The Kiltartan Poetry Book* (1918) continues an Irish theme even while Yeats's mind was elsewhere. Then there is a pair of books, *Poems* by Thomas Parnell (1927) and Mario Rossi's *Pilgrimage in the West* (1933) that reflects Yeats's 'discovery' of the Irish eighteenth century. Yeats was not of an excluding mind. Where a humbler vision might see only disparity, his could hold diverse periods and personalities until they achieved reconciliation, and in this may lie the ultimate unity for the series of books from Dun Emer and Cuala.

III THE OXFORD BOOK OF MODERN VERSE

I

With *The Oxford Book of Modern Verse* (1936) Yeats found a new audience for his edited work. The publications from Cuala (including the *Broadsides*), given the limitations of a small private press, could reach only a relatively few readers. With the resources of the Oxford University Press, Yeats was assured of a much larger audience, Irish, English, and American, and this must have been one of the attractions of the *Oxford Book* for him.

Yeats was in fact the second editor to take on the Oxford anthology. The first, Lascelles Abercrombie, the English poet, gave up the project after four years, realizing that he might lose his reputation and a good number of friends deciding what poets belonged in the anthology.[104] Yeats had no such reservations. His reputation as a critic *was* in fact tarnished in making the *Oxford Book* though as a great poet he survived it, while he included enough of his friends in the anthology to prevent their defection.

The Oxford University Press had at first considered a variety of writers to succeed Abercrombie; Yeats was always an attractive possibility, but also on the list were Eliot, De La Mare, Graves, Huxley, and Herbert Read. A number of them were more likely to be familiar with strictly contemporary poetry, but all had liabilities. Eliot was committed to Faber and Faber (who were bringing out their own anthology of Modern poetry) and Humphrey Milford, publisher to the Delegates of the Oxford University Press, thought he 'would be perverse and obstinate', while De La Mare, he suspected, 'would feel it his duty to be whimsical'. Huxley seemed 'unsuitable', while Herbert Read had offended another Clarendon Press anthologist, Quiller-Couch, in a review of *The Oxford Book of English Poetry*. Graves seemed unacceptable.[105] This left Yeats the strongest contender; he was approached and accepted the task of making the *Oxford Book*. This was sometime between the middle of October and early November 1934. As a London editor of the Press wrote: Yeats 'has a "modern" manner, is admired by the moderns, and his name will last when he is dead.'[106] There is no indication that anyone at the Press consulted Yeats's previously edited work, though it might have told them much about what they could expect in the *Oxford Book* forestalling some surprises. Nor did they ask him, it seems, however discretely, what he thought of Modern poetry. Undoubtedly, the tendency then as now was to see Modernism as monolithic, but of course there were some fractures.

Why did Yeats accept the *Oxford Book*? He was after all sixty-nine, not in good health, and not very familiar with contemporary English and American poetry. Of course he did it for the money, but that is an obvious reason. Yeats also thought it might help his own work. As he wrote Dorothy Wellesley, 'I began this volume of selections . . . that I might be reborn in imagination.'[107] His other letters to Dorothy Wellesley show Yeats casting about for new directions for his own poetry; reading for the *Oxford Book* would give him a chance to find out what younger poets were doing, and their youthfulness might be contagious. These were positive personal reasons. The anthology also gave Yeats a chance to evaluate Modern poetry and to decide his relationship to it. This promised to be more polemical.

As Yeats wrote to Margot Ruddock in February 1935:

> I am trying to understand for the sake of my *Cambridge* [sic] *Book of Modern Verse* the Auden, Eliot school. I do not mean to give it a great deal of space, but must define my objections to it, and I cannot know this till I see clearly what quality it has [that has] made it delight young Cambridge and young Oxford.[108]

There was surely another reason for doing the anthology, not often stated but frequently implied in his letters of this period: to oppose to the 'Ezra, Eliot, Auden school' (as he called it elsewhere) another tradition of poetry, his own, as he thought, and that of some poets in Ireland and a few English allies. Yeats was imprecise in sweeping Pound, Eliot, and Auden into one 'school', but the qualities in their work he was opposing to his own 'school' (again a very wide net) were elaborated in a letter to Dorothy Wellesley:

> This difficult work, which is being written everywhere now . . . has the substance of philosophy & is a delight to the poet with

his professional pattern; but it is not your road or mine, & ours is the main road, the road of naturalness & swiftness and we have thirty centuries upon our side. We alone can "think like a wise man, yet express our selves like the common people". These new men are goldsmiths working with a glass screwed into one eye, whereas we stride ahead of the crowd, its swordsmen, its jugglers, looking to right & left. "To right and left" by which I mean that we need like Milton, Shakespeare, Shelley, vast sentiments, generalizations supported by tradition.[109]

'My anthology should be the standard anthology for some time',[110] he told Margot Ruddock, and through it he hoped he could counter what he disliked in contemporary poetry by opposing to it the poetry of the 'main road'. The *Oxford Book* would define this tradition in more detail.

Inevitably, when Yeats began planning the anthology he wanted some changes. His contract with the Oxford University Press had stipulated that the selection should 'contain poems representative of the period nineteen hundred and thirty-five by British, Irish and American poets.'[111] But Yeats decided (with the publisher's assent) that he would begin at Tennyson's death so that he could show a development to the poetry of the 1930's. Initially Yeats had wanted to include American poets and Humphrey Milford had agreed ('they have, we think, more and better of the Modernist lot than England'),[112] but Yeats finally was persuaded by T. S. Eliot to include only the handful of Americans whose work he knew and liked personally; this was modified further in the anthology to those American poets who had lived in Europe for a long time or whose subjects were European (Yeats did not elaborate on what these might be). Actually, Yeats had found that he did not like much American poetry, but he thought it might hurt sales in the United States if he admitted this in the book itself.[113]

Throughout the spring and summer of 1935 Yeats read poetry preliminary to making his selection for the *Oxford Book*, adding many volumes to his own library, eventually slicing out pages to get preliminary copy just as he had done in making Dorothy Wellesley's *Selections*. Less accessible works he consulted at the British Museum;

as he reported to A. P. Watt, his agent, at one session in London he 'read or smelt 45 books of poetry'.[114] In his reading he found some new enthusiasms, Dorothy Wellesley, W. J. Turner, a British music critic and poet, Edith Sitwell (not entirely new) and Elynor Wylie. All except the last (an American) got extensive coverage in Yeats's final selection as well as in his Introduction. Along the way, he found out that Faber and Faber were also planning an anthology of Modern poetry; he wrote to the London editor of the Oxford University Press, 'we are apparently in for a war of the books'.[115] To Dorothy Wellesley he confided that he had heard that its contents would be 'ultra-radical'.[116] If there was in fact a race to publish, the Oxford anthology was outstripped by *The Faber Book of Modern Verse* published in February 1936, a more orthodox selection of Modern poetry than Yeats's was to be and not nearly as 'ultra-radical' as he had perhaps feared.

Yeats finished his selection in November 1935[117] but the contents of the anthology were not delivered to the Press until late April of 1936 ('Some queer stuff, but perhaps as popular as we could expect' was Milford's reaction, though not to Yeats).[118] Mrs. Yeats had taken on the drudgery of typing contents, seeing to acknowledgments, and paying authors. During the spring and summer of 1936 while Yeats was in Majorca helping the Swami make his translations from the Upanishads, Mrs. Yeats became in fact the sub-editor, seeing, for example, that a later version of one of Herbert Trench's poems was used in the anthology, adding a note to a poem by Thomas McGreevy, and negotiating with the Oxford University Press.[119]

II

After considerable confusion about acknowledgments that had not been made to authors and publishers, *The Oxford Book of Modern Verse* was published on 19 November 1936. The publishers had asked for, and got, a long Introduction by Yeats. It is, on the whole, a very personal chronological view of the period from 1892 to 1935. Though in the first sections Yeats uses various personae, a young man beginning an intellectual life in the late Eighties, a young poet coming under Pater's influence, this is, initially at least, a chronicle of Yeats's

The Oxford Book Of Modern Verse
1892–1935

Chosen by
W. B. Yeats

Oxford
At the Clarendon Press
1936

development. He emphasizes his relationship with the Rhymers' Club and their reaction against Victorian rhetoric and the 'impurities' of 'irrelevant nature description', 'scientific and moral discursiveness' and 'political eloquence'. The poets of 'The Cheshire Cheese' shied away from political and social movements 'convinced that to take part in such movements would be only less disgraceful than to write for the newspapers' (in fact Yeats had done both).[120] The reaction against Victorian rhetoric begun by the poets of the Nineties was continued elsewhere. In Ireland the folk movement employed the ballad rather than the lyric of the Rhymers, but it too was reacting against Victorian discursiveness ('an old ballad is never rhetorical', Yeats wrote) and the Irish movement had its counterpart in the poetry of Housman, Hardy, and to an extent Kipling.

By 1900 Victorianism was overthrown, Yeats believed, but English poetry continued on traditional themes in the ballad (Masefield), the short lyric (Bridges) or in the more fanciful poetry of Laurence Binyon and T. Sturge Moore. 'None of these were innovators; they preferred to keep all the past their rival.'[121] This was an important admission, for Yeats, unlike Michael Roberts, editor of the Faber anthology, did not demand that his poets advance poetic technique.

With the Great War, Yeats thought, came a distinct break in English poetry, one that he largely regretted. To explain it, he had to reach back beyond the Victorian period to the end of the seventeenth century 'when men became passive before a mechanized nature'.[122] (The quality of 'passivity' is a central point in Yeats's criticism of Modern poetry.) The artist becomes merely a receptor, literature turns realistic, the subject is the 'flux' of external phenomena. T. S. Eliot, according to Yeats, after rejecting Romantic 'rhythms and metaphors' felt required to accept a realistic, contemporary subject matter, Paddington railway station rather than Tristram and Iseult.[123] Pound 'made flux his theme'; at its worst his poetry becomes 'nervous obsession, nightmare, stammering confusion'.[124] From Eliot, Yeats traces the line of Modern English poetry directly through the war poets to Auden, Spender, MacNeice, and Day Lewis, the youngest writers on the scene.

Yeats was obviously discouraged by what he saw of English poetry in 1935. Nevertheless, he was attracted to a group of English 'philosophical' poets, W. J. Turner, Herbert Read, and Dorothy Wellesley who (intuitively at least) rejected passivity and asserted, Yeats thought, that the 'flux' is of the perceiving mind itself. For these writers (and he tentatively adds Eliot of *The Waste Land*) 'what we call the solid earth was manufactured by the human mind from unknown raw material.'[125] He gave Turner, Read, and Wellesley generous coverage in the anthology, Eliot somewhat less. Yeats thought that Irish poetry continued unchecked by English developments following the war. 'Instead of turning to impersonal philosophy', Irish poets 'hardened and deepened their personalities'. Oliver Gogarty still celebrated individuality in the lyric and other Irish poets still wrote the ballads that tied them to a living folk tradition.[126] These two strains of English and Irish poetry constituted the 'main road' that Yeats had pointed out to Dorothy Wellesley and one function of the *Oxford Book* was to give them a fitting display.

III

Yeats's Introduction certainly prepares for the selection that follows, but there is still the unexpected. Fully a third of the poets included were dead by the date of the anthology; in fact a significant number did not live past the war. Admittedly Yeats had given some notice of this intention ('Even a long-lived man has the right to call his own generation modern'[127]) and it was within the terms of agreement with the Oxford University Press.

Yeats had only discussed Irish poetry briefly in his Introduction, but there were a large number of Irish poets included, though a few did not have an obvious Irish label. Many were Cuala authors and the poems Yeats chose from them tend to be from Cuala editions. In the Irish selections there are the expected emphases, on the ballad, on translations from the Gaelic, on 'peasant' subject matter and the Kiltartan English developed by Hyde, Lady Gregory, and Synge. Many of the poems use subjects from Irish mythology or Irish history. If the reader expected all these poets to write like Yeats, he was surprised. There is a real diversity of style and subject from Æ to Gogarty to Higgins. Nevertheless, there is a single impression that is the result of Yeats's selection rather than the poetry itself. Yeats included poets in the anthology according to their dates of birth, but within each selection he attempted, as he wrote Dorothy Wellesley, 'unity of effect'.[128] In Lady Gregory's translations, in 'Cold, Sharp Lamentation' and 'A Poem written in Time of Trouble', for example, the predominant mood is melancholic, one of hardship and regret. This feeling is continued in other selections as well, in the translations by Frank O'Connor, in 'A Grey Eye Weeping' and 'Kilcash', though it is counterpointed by the more astringent 'Prayer for the Speedy End of Three Great Misfortunes'. This much might be attributed to the nature of the Irish originals. Nevertheless, in Synge's own poetry there is still this strong elegiac mood, a sense of death and defeat unrelieved by Synge's more Rabelaisian manner (his ballads are surprisingly missing). The poems by other Irishmen are largely in this vein too, those by Colum, Higgins, McGreevy, Rolleston, and Stephens, even an occasional poem by Gogarty ('Non Dolet'). There is no indication that Yeats intended to emphasize this mood in Irish poetry; in fact he seems to have been surprised by it himself. As he wrote to Dorothy Wellesley: 'Now that I have had all my Anthology in galley proofs I am astonished at the greatness of much of the poetry, & its sadness.'[129] While Yeats says that his wife chose his own selection[130] (though surely with his approval), the mood of his poems in the anthology mirrors that of the other Irish poets and in a way responds to it. The subjects too are old age, death, political disillusionment, the destruction of the aristocratic tradition in Ireland, but the ultimate mood is not dejection. Yeats's response in 'To a Friend whose Work has come to Nothing' is typical: in the face of defeat and disintegration the proper response is 'exultation', 'Because of all things known / That is the most difficult'. Yeats made clear elsewhere that this was, he thought, the solution of tragedy, and it seems fitting that he (or Mrs. Yeats) should end his selection with an excerpt from his translation of *Oedipus at Colonus*. In his Introduction Yeats asserted, in a discussion of the English war poets, that 'passive suffering is not a theme for poetry' and his own selection in the *Oxford Book* seems to affirm that principle.

In Yeats's selection from English poets, the work of the Rhymers' Club is generously represented (they had, after all, pointed the way in removing Victorian 'impurities' from poetry) though by no means are all the members represented. But Yeats's choice of poems is somewhat untypical. After reading it one has the impression that the Rhymers' Club was largely a devotional society; the decadent element is almost entirely missing. There is a distinct strain of religious or mystical poetry running through the anthology, from Francis Thompson to Tagore, Shri Purohit Swami, and Margot Ruddock, and Yeats may have been emphasizing this in the Rhymers as well. It would have been interesting to see what Yeats might have selected from John Gray, his religious or decadent poetry, but his estate refused permission.

Much of the other work leading up to the 'Moderns' (Yeats did not include himself under this term), and it is a large proportion of the anthology, is quite obviously simple, unintellectual poetry. Many of these poems are songs, ballads, ballad adaptations, or use ballad devices such as the refrain. But Yeats could defend this selection. The editors of the Clarendon Press hoped they were getting a popular anthology, and Yeats was conscious of this in making the *Oxford Book*, as when he decided against a bawdy translation by Gogarty because 'it would exclude the book from school libraries'.[131] But Yeats did not have to condescend to make a popular selection. His own work on the Cuala *Broadsides* was intended to develop a popular poetry for Ireland, and he himself practised the ballad in his later poetry, though admittedly with more skill than is always found in the Oxford anthology. As Yeats was fond of saying to Dorothy Wellesley, 'We alone can "think like a wise man, yet express ourselves like the common people".'[132] At another time when the rhythm of a poem by Dorothy Wellesley in the anthology had been criticised as simplistic, he wrote her that it was 'merely the dance music of the ages',[133] and this can be taken as his apology for other uncomplex poetry in the *Oxford Book*. And yet a number of poems in the anthology remain puzzling, long unimpressive poems by Laurence Binyon, Ralph Hodgson, and T. Sturge Moore, though in the last case friendship certainly determined that the selection would be substantial. These poems do not seem that important now. Yeats underestimated some other poets.

Yeats's preconceptions about T. S. Eliot largely determined the selection he made from him for the *Oxford Book*. His assessment seems to stem from some isolated qualities in some isolated poems. Eliot 'has described men and women that get out of bed or into it from mere habit' [134] and thus we get 'Preludes'. Eliot is primarily a 'satirist' so Yeats includes 'Sweeney among the Nightingales', 'The Hippopotamus', and *The Hollow Men*. Yeats wrote to Dorothy Wellesley that 'The worst language is Elliot's [sic] in all his early poems — a level flatness of rhythm',[135] a judgment repeated in more polite terms in his Introduction. Yeats thought his language more animated in *The Hollow Men* and *Ash-Wednesday*, but at the same time he did not like Eliot's religious sense, declaring that there was 'little self-surrender in his personal relation to God and the soul',[136] so he excludes *Ash-Wednesday* from his choice, leaving a selection largely from the earlier work that he disliked. He does include 'Journey of the Magi', though probably more for its speech rhythms than its religious content. In general though, it is not a selection critics more attuned to Eliot would agree with.

Pound might have fared better if Yeats had included his original selection for the *Oxford Book*, but he found Pound's poems 'too expensive', and he apologized for the limited selection at the end of his Introduction. He put in only three poems: 'The River-merchant's Wife: a Letter', an excerpt from 'Homage to Sextus Propertius' and 'Canto XVII', all exemplifying that 'deliberate nobility' that had come in for careful praise in his Introduction. Some other poems Yeats had chosen initially show more diverse qualities, the casual irreverence of 'The Lake Isle' (Pound often brought Yeats into his poems), sarcasm in section V of *Hugh Selwyn Mauberley* ('There died a myriad . . . For an old bitch gone in the teeth'), or Pound's distant approximation of the folk ('A Ballad of the Mulberry Road').[137] There is no indication that Yeats intended to include more than the single 'Canto XVII', since he considered the *Cantos* doubtful experiments, 'merely exquisite or grotesque fragments'.[138]

Yeats was less certain of the poetry of Auden, C. Day Lewis, Spender, and MacNeice. He seems to have been more excited by it than he had expected. Their energy and commitment attracted him more than Eliot's scrupulous meanness (as he thought it); he granted them 'intellectual passion' but he also thought they had inherited

Pound's obscurity and lack of form.[139] His selections from their work are often uncomprehending. Auden may have been thinking of his own selection in the *Oxford Book* when he called the anthology 'the most deplorable volume ever issued' from the Clarendon Press.[140] Its very perfunctoriness must have seemed an insult, only four poems and one of these may have been included by mistake.[141] 'It's no use raising a shout' must have seemed to Yeats typical of the new colloquialism in poetry, but it was not one of Auden's best poems (he left it out of his *Collected Shorter Poems*). On the other hand, 'This lunar beauty' is an impressive enough lyric, but one has to go to MacNeice to find Auden's characteristic persona (in 'An Ecloque for Christmas'). In fact MacNeice and C. Day Lewis do better in the anthology than Auden; MacNeice was an Irishman by birth, an anti-Communist (or so Yeats thought), and his poetry was more accessible than Auden's though more imitative too (besides having elements of Auden, his 'Ecloque' in the anthology is a Yeatsian dialogue of the divided self). C. Day Lewis gets a fairly typical selection, though most of the pieces are from his earlier *Transitional Poem* rather than the later, more ideological *The Magnetic Mountain*.

While Yeats scanted the 'Ezra, Eliot, Auden school' in the anthology, he gave extravagant selections from Edith Sitwell, Dorothy Wellesley, Oliver Gogarty, and W. J. Turner, hardly a 'school' themselves as Yeats contended, but poets at least without other attachments and thus free to enter into one at Yeats's suggestion. Though Edith Sitwell's poetry shared qualities with that of Eliot, Pound, and Auden—fragmentation, dislocation of language, and obscurity, Yeats thought it saved by a 'powerful, artifical vividness'[142] (all three terms carry weight), presumably evidence of an active rather than a passive mind. Dorothy Wellesley, Gogarty, and Turner, though very different kinds of poets, came in for the same measured praise from Yeats. Wellesley had 'lucky eyes', a gift of intuition, Turner had occasional 'precision', Gogarty wrote 'heroic song', but all could be careless poets, little given to revision (Yeats often helped here). Dorothy Wellesley often drifted into irrelevance or obscurity, Gogarty wrote 'first drafts of poems rather than poems', Turner 'After clearing up some metaphysical obscurity' 'leaves obscure what a moment's thought would have cleared.'[143] But these were the preliminary reservations; Yeats liked their poetry immensely.

While Yeats considered Wellesley and Turner 'philosophical poets' the label is difficult to apply. They may at times have struck off lines that tantalized Yeats by confirming conclusions he had come to independently, but they were not hard thinkers. Virginia Sackville-West, Dorothy Wellesley's good friend, made what seems a harsh but fair assessment of the philosophy in her poetry: 'she often imposed upon her verse a weight it should never have been asked to carry. She felt; she saw; she interpreted. Her undoing as a poet, sometimes, was that she thought she could think.'[144] For all that Yeats said about Turner's philosophy, he seems, at least from the evidence of the poems he quotes in his letters, more deeply moved by Turner's poetry describing his attitude and relationship to women as in 'The Word made Flesh' and 'Hymn to her Unknown'.

Yeats considered Gogarty a great lyricist, a contemporary link with the kind of poetry the Rhymers made, an art he thought neglected in 1935. Yeats was attracted to poetry written out of personality rather than impersonality, and in Gogarty he found a multi-faceted individual, 'scholar, wit, poet, gay adventurer'.[145] Then too, Yeats thought he needed Gogarty's poetry: it provided a classical check for the Romantic element in his own poetry with its 'sense of a hardship borne and chosen out of pride and joy', its 'astringent' adjectives, its description of competent warriors and beautiful tragic women as in the poem 'Portrait with Background'.[146] These may not seem like the qualities an anthologist should select for, but Yeats thought so. He included seventeen poems by Gogarty in the *Oxford Book*, though many are quite short. However just or unjust this number may be in respect to other poets in the anthology, the poems included show that when he was sympathetic Yeats could make a very good selection.

IV

Yeats had fourteen poems in the *Oxford Book* under his own name, but there was more of his work in the anthology than most readers could know. Yeats very publicly trimmed the 'foreign feathers' from Oscar Wilde's *The Ballad of Reading Gaol* (he acknowledged cutting Wilde's poem in his Introduction), but Yeats's revisions go beyond this. The editors at the Oxford University Press quickly got used to the freedom Yeats allowed himself with his authors. When he sent them only two stanzas of Housman's 'Soldier Rest Thy Warfare Over' they accepted this as an instance of Yeats's revision, but they asked Yeats just to be sure. It was in fact a mistake and Yeats restored the missing stanzas, cutting back further on Wilde's ballad to make room for them.[147] In another case of a well known poet, Yeats, troubled by an inversion in a line from Pound's 'The River-merchant's Wife: a Letter', changed 'At fourteen I married My Lord you' to 'At fourteen we were married to one another'[148] (thinking that Pound should have learned that lesson long before), but he must have thought better of it, for Pound's original line stands in the *Oxford Book*. Yeats took more freedom with less public texts.

In the anthology Yeats has altered work by not only Wilde but Tagore, Wellesley, Turner, Higgins, O'Connor and Gogarty. Admittedly many of the revisions were not made specifically for the Oxford anthology. Yeats had collaborated on O'Connor's translations 'A Grey Eye Weeping' and 'Kilcash' for their Cuala publication. Gogarty has acknowledged Yeats's help with 'Palinode' but it too had been published before at Cuala in the same version.[149] The revisions in Dorothy Wellesley's poems ('Lenin' for example) were carried over from her *Selections*, those from Tagore came mainly from *Gitanjali*, both Yeats editions.

F. R. Higgins's 'The Ballad of O'Bruadir' had already appeared in a version Yeats had altered for *Broadsides* (1935), but he changed it further to accelerate the narrative. 'In narrative verse we want to concentrate the attention on the fact or the story',[150] Yeats had written, and this explains not only this revision, but the much more drastic pruning of Wilde's ballad. 'I plucked out even famous lines because, effective in themselves, put into the Ballad they become artificial, trivial, arbitrary', Yeats explained.[151] The meaning of the ballad must develop from the narrative; 'rapidity' must not be checked by meditation or soliloquy. Though Yeats accentuated both the ballad and 'philosophical' poetry in the *Oxford Book*, he did not want them confused. The ballad must retain spontaneity, just as he had insisted on this quality in another popular form, the folk tale, in 1888.

W. J. Turner wrote a very different kind of poetry, but it too came in for extensive revision in the anthology. Turner could write some excellent lines and stanzas, but not often completely satisfying poems. Yeats found this in Turner's *Songs and Incantations*:

> For the blood of a man when he is old
> Old and full of power,
> Is no longer like the blood of a young man, inflammable,
> Is like a serpent and an eagle,
> A bull violent and immovable,
> And a burning that is without flame or substance

but Turner mars the passage by adding a vague analogy: 'Like the burning of the holy bush / Or the lock of Satan'. Yeats has removed these similes and a few others like them in the version of this poem 'The Word Made Flesh?' in the anthology, as well as commonplace lines and tautologies, improving the poem considerably. Though Turner later seemed to repudiate Yeats's revisions in this poem, his *Selected Poems* (1939) follows them closely.[152] In Turner's other poems for the *Oxford Book*, Yeats has revised the final line of 'Reflection' (Turner thought it ruined the poem), removed the last four stanzas of 'Epithalamium' (they blur the poem), and drastically rearranged the sections from Turner's *The Seven Days of the Sun* (lines and stanzas have been cut here too).

Not all Yeats's revisions in the anthology were stylistic. In Dorothy Wellesley's 'Lenin', a description of her visit to the tomb of the revolutionary in 1927, Yeats has cut a digressive beginning and ending, but he has also changed Dorothy Wellesley's description of Lenin, 'Much writing these delicate hands have done' to 'Many warrants these delicate hands have signed'.[153] Yeats's revision is more concrete, but it alters the tone of the original, adding an ominous note when Dorothy Wellesley's reaction in the full poem was more complex. Such revisions — with ideological overtones — are rare. Yeats's practice of revising his fellow authors was, as we have seen, a very old one. It was in some cases Yeats's unusual method of appreciating their work. In the *Oxford Book* Yeats certainly wanted the poetry of Turner, Wellesley, and Higgins to fulfil the expectations of his Introduction; his revisions could help, but their work, despite this, remains distinctively their own.

The Oxford Book of Modern Verse was very widely reviewed, not surprising for a popular anthology by a noted poet from a prestigious publisher. Many of the reviewers were disapproving, and undoubtedly they would have been more severe had Yeats's revisions been known. As it was, the reviewers fastened largely on his selection. No omission caused more uproar than that of Wilfred Owen. Yeats seemed genuinely surprised by the vehemence of the reaction, though he should have been warned through his correspondence with the editors of the Oxford University Press (who thought readers would expect Owen) and through Dorothy Wellesley's repeated attempts to get him into the anthology (she had included Owen and other war poets in her own *A Broadcast Anthology of Modern Poetry* in 1930). Much has been written about Yeats's principle that 'passive suffering is not a theme for poetry' and its application to Owen's poetry. A few points need emphasis. 'Passivity' was not a term invented by Yeats solely to keep Owen out of the anthology, but is applied more widely in his Introduction, though always pejoratively. Yeats did not exclude all war poetry from the anthology, nor is it all of one type. Balanced against Grenfell's hymn to combat, 'Into Battle,' is Sassoon's bitter 'On Passing the New Menin Gate', though it is the only example of its kind. It would have been even more in the minority if Yeats had included an initial selection of nine of Robert Nichols's fairly complacent war poems, but he used some later poems instead.[154] Unfortunately Owen had become identified in Yeats's mind (even before the publication of the *Oxford Book*) with 'Communist' critics who had, in one instance anyway, used Owen against Yeats, and he could not (or would not) see past them to Owen himself.[155]

Yeats had often been accused before of making unrepresentative editions, and at first he revelled in the hostile reaction to the anthology as a sign that 'I have some where got down to reality'.[156] Eventually he was more affected. After attacks from Liberals accusing him of slighting the Moderns, from Conservatives accusing him of giving in to them, from the Irish complaining that he had included the wrong Irish poets, and the Americans that he had not included enough Americans, Yeats admitted to Dorothy Wellesley a feeling of exhaustion, and he assigned one cause: 'Attacks on Anthology (Feeling that I have no nation, that somebody has bitten my apple all around)'.[157] At least he could be satisfied that the anthology was selling well; he had found a popular audience.

Though *The Oxford Book of Modern Verse* went through many editions (the Clarendon Press was still printing 3,000 copies in 1951),[158] Yeats's larger hopes for the *Oxford Book* failed. Traditional, uncomplicated poetry written to 'the dance music of the ages' did not reassert itself against difficult introspective work, contemporary subjects and realistic rhythms. Turner did not replace Eliot in the English syllabus, nor is Dorothy Wellesley remembered very much except perhaps as Yeats's correspondent of later life. With Yeats's death that odd coalition of a handful of Irish poets, a titled Englishwoman, and a British music critic who wrote poetry broke up. It is unlikely that very many people knew it happened. To Yeats the schools had confronted one another, but most critics continued to see the *Oxford Book* as a shameless act of favouritism from a great poet to some lesser ones. Yeats's attempt to promote popular poetry moved back from the Oxford University Press to Cuala (for the 1937 *Broadsides*) and then briefly to the studio of the BBC for a series of poetry broadcasts, but garbled transmissions and the difficulties of reconciling words and music ended that experiment. Yeats died frustrated in his hopes for changing the direction of Modern poetry. He was not alone in his frustration. Many poets left the Thirties with a sense of failure, but Yeats for one had a place for this defeat in his understanding and in his poetry.

APPENDIX: SUGGESTED ADDITIONS TO 'BOOKS EDITED BY YEATS' IN ALLAN WADE'S *A BIBLIOGRAPHY OF THE WRITINGS OF W. B. YEATS*

Æ (George Russell), *The Nuts of Knowledge*. Dublin: The Dun Emer Press, 1903.*

Æ, *By Still Waters*. Dublin: The Dun Emer Press, 1906.

J. M. Synge, *Works of John M. Synge, Poems, Translations from Petrarch, Translations from Villon and others*, II. Dublin: Maunsel and Co., 1910.

Rabindranath Tagore, *Gitanjali*. London: The India Society, 1912.

Rabindranath Tagore, *The Gardener*. London: Macmillan and Co., 1913. [Edited with T. Sturge Moore.]

Oliver Gogarty, *An Offering of Swans*. Dublin: The Cuala Press, 1923.

Oliver Gogarty, *Wild Apples*. Dublin: The Cuala Press, 1930.

Frank O'Connor, *The Wild Bird's Nest*. Dublin: The Cuala Press, 1932.

Shri Purohit Swami, *An Indian Monk*. London: Macmillan and Co., 1932. [Edited with T. Sturge Moore.]

Bhagwan Shri Hamsa, *The Holy Mountain*, translated by Shri Purohit Swami. London: Faber and Faber, 1934.

Dorothy Wellesley, *Selections from the Poems of Dorothy Wellesley*. London: Macmillan and Co., 1936.

Margot Ruddock, *The Lemon Tree*. London: J. M. Dent, 1937.

Bhagwan Shree Patanjali, *Aphorisms of Yoga*, translated by Shree Purohit Swami. London: Faber and Faber, 1938.

Frank O'Connor, *Lords and Commons*. Dublin: The Cuala Press, 1938.

*As general editorial advisor to the Dun Emer and Cuala Press, W. B. Yeats generally had control over what books went into the series. However, for this volume and the others listed from the Press, he had more particular editorial responsibility, either for selecting or revising contents or both.

NOTES ON THE TEXT

1. Though Yeats probably helped with the editing of another book the same year, *Poems and Ballads of Young Ireland*, the evidence points to a group effort of John and Ellen O'Leary, Katharine Tynan, and Yeats. See *The Letters of W. B. Yeats*, edited by Allan Wade. London 1954. p. 37 note; subsequent references to this volume will be made in the text as *Letters*. This treatment of *Fairy and Folk Tales* appeared in *Southern Folklore Quarterly* in an expanded form.
2. *Autobiographies* by W. B. Yeats. London, 1955. p. 149. *Memoirs* by W. B. Yeats, edited by Denis Donoghue. New York, 1973. p. 32.
3. *Fairy and Folk Tales of the Irish Peasantry* by W. B. Yeats. London, 1888. p. xvi.
4. *Ibid.*, p. xiv.
5. *Legendary Fictions of the Irish Celts* by Patrick Kennedy. London, 1866. p. ix.
6. *Fairy and Folk Tales*, p. xv.
7. *The Dublin and London Magazine*. October 1825. pp. 352-4.
8. *Ibid.*, March 1825. p. 31.
9. *Beside the Fire* by Douglas Hyde. London, 1890. p. xi.
10. *The Poor Scholar and Other Tales* by William Carleton. Dublin, 1869. pp. 200-10. In this case I have considered an edition published in the same year as the author's death the definitive edition for comparative purposes. In subsequent collations I have followed the practice of using the latest edition before Yeats's edition that was available. I have also consulted every other available edition of the works discussed to determine that they do not duplicate the unique features of Yeats's text. Of course, this excludes editions later than Yeats's which may have used *his* editions as a source.
11. *Ibid.*, p. 231.
12. *Ibid.*, p. 225.
13. *Uncollected Prose* by W. B. Yeats, edited by John P. Frayne. New York, 1970. p. 187.
14. *The Irish Novelists: 1800-1850* by Thomas Flanagan. New York, 1959. p. 36.
15. *Fairy and Folk Tales*, p. xv.
16. *Legends and Stories of Ireland* by Samuel Lover. London, 1837. p. 4.
17. The list of authorities repeats for the most part that in *Fairy and Folk Tales* with the addition of Jeremiah Curtin, Hyde, and David Fitzgerald, that is, the new scientific school of folklorists. It also shows evidence of Yeats's intense reading of the Irish novelists for *Representative Irish Tales*.

18 *Legends and Stories of Ireland*, pp. 141-56; *History of Ireland*, I, by Standish O'Grady. London, 1878. pp. 127-9; *The Wonders of Ireland* by P. W. Joyce. London, 1911. pp. 184-5.
19 *Uncollected Prose*, p. 143.
20 Lough Derg ('Patrick's Purgatory'), a lake in Co. Donegal and a popular shrine to St. Patrick.
21 *Stories from Carleton*, edited by W. B. Yeats. London, 1889. pp. 200-39.
22 Quoted in *Uncollected Prose*, p. 166.
23 *Ibid.*, pp. 167-9.
24 Berg Collection, New York Public Library. Quoted with permission. The *Nation* review had, it seems, been transformed into 'a long letter' in Yeats's memory in 1901. The 'office' is presumably that of *The Nation*.
25 Quoted in *A Bibliography of the Writings of W. B. Yeats* by Allan Wade. London 1968. p. 237.
26 *The Irish Monthly*. July 1891. p. 379.
27 *The Saturday Review*, London. 30 May 1891. p. 664.
28 *Ibid.*
29 *The Academy*. 10 October 1891. pp. 306-7.
30 *The Irish Monthly*. July 1891. p. 379.
31 *Blackwoods*. May 1838. pp. 614-7.
32 *Uncollected Prose*, p. 241.
33 *A Book of Irish Verse* edited by W. B. Yeats. London 1895. p. xxvii.
34 For a full discussion of the Yeats-Duffy book scheme controversy, see *Yeats and the Beginning of the Irish Renaissance* by Phillip L. Marcus. Ithaca 1970. pp. 98-100.
35 *A Book of Irish Verse*. London, 1900. p. xiii.
36 *Ibid.*, 1895. p. xxvi.
37 *Ibid.*, p. xiii.
38 *Ibid.*, p. xviii.
39 *Ibid.*, p. xviii; 1900 edition, p. xxiii.
40 *Ibid.*, 1900. p. xxviii.
41 *Ibid.*, 1895. p. xxv.
42 *Ibid.*, p. 250.
43 *The Poetical Works of Gerald Griffin*. Dublin 1926. p. 162.
44 *Ibid.*, p. 163. Yeats also excluded these lines in the version of the poem in *Fairy and Folk Tales*.
45 See *The Complete Poems of Lionel Johnson*, edited by Iain Fletcher. London 1953. p. 327.
46 Berg Collection, New York Public Library. Used with permission. The 'expensive anthology' is *A Treasury of Irish Poetry* (1900).
47 Yeats proposed this specific substitution in a further letter to Methuen on 27 August. Berg Collection.
48 Though Yeats contributed introductory material to *Irish Literature*, he

specifically disclaimed any editorial involvement with the anthology. See *Letters*, 415-6.
49 This arrangement of a limited expensive edition followed by a popular edition (in this case in 'The Muses' Library') became a common practice with Yeats. Ellis published his own edition of Blake in 1906.
50 This discussion is indebted to *Blake in the Nineteenth Century* by Deborah Dorfman, New Haven 1969, and *Blake and Yeats* by Hazard Adams. New York 1955. pp. 44-56.
51 Berg Collection, New York Public Library. Used with permission.
52 *The Works of William Blake*, III, edited by Edwin John Ellis and William Butler Yeats. London 1893. p. 88.
53 *The Poems of William Blake*, edited by W. B. Yeats. London 1893. p. 261.
54 *Poems of Spenser*, edited by W. B. Yeats. Edinburgh 1906. p. xviii.
55 *Ibid.*, p. xxviii.
56 *Ibid.*, p. xxxiii.
57 *Ibid.*, p. xliv.
58 'Beltaine', the Irish festival of spring coincided with the first performances of the Irish Literary Theatre; the name was changed to 'Samhain' (winter) when the performances were moved to the end of the year — also to indicate that the Irish Theatre, as Yeats felt, had entered a mature phase. *The Arrow* concerned itself mainly with the controversy over Synge's *Playboy of the Western World*.
59 The third number of *Beltaine* had only Yeats's short assessment of the Irish Literary Theatre through February, 1900. It was written at the publisher's request to round out the *Beltaine* series for permanent publication (*Letters*, 334-5).
60 *Beltaine*. February 1900. p. 6.
61 As summarized by Yeats in *Samhain*. 1902. pp. 9-10.
62 *Certain Noble Plays of Japan*, edited by Ezra Pound. Dublin 1916. p. 1.
63 Most editions ran 200 - 400 copies; 10 shillings was an average price.
64 *A Book of Irish Verse*, 1900. pp. xiii-xiv.
65 See *Letters*, 232 note; this book was announced for Cuala, but it must have been left over from Dun Emer.
66 Yeats also tended to select early rather than contemporary work from the living authors in the Dun Emer list. The reasons were various. Æ and Katharine Tynan were beginning to repeat themselves in their poetry, while Douglas Hyde, Yeats thought, had neglected his poetry in propagandizing for the Gaelic League. John Eglinton, still a vigorous essayist when Yeats made *Some Essays and Passages By John Eglinton* in 1905, formally protested Yeats's choice of early material in a note to that volume.

67 Most of the poems were collected from *Celtic Christmas*, a supplement to *The Irish Homestead*. Yeats thought it the epitome of amateur poetry. See *Letters*, 473-4.
68 *New Songs*, edited by Æ. Dublin 1904. p. 5.
69 *The Dun Emer Press, later The Cuala Press* by Liam Miller. Dublin 1973. p. 38.
70 This excerpt has been edited out of the letter to Miss Tynan in Wade's *Letters*, pp. 476-8. It has been added from a typescript in the Harvard University Library. Used by permission.
71 *Letters from Æ*, edited by Alan Denson. London 1961. p. xiii.
72 But Yeats did edit the posthumous Maunsel edition, adding five poems from Synge's manuscripts and six translations. In the additional poems interest centres on certain discrepancies between Synge's manuscripts (as presented in the Oxford edition edited by Robin Skelton) and the printed versions. These range from punctuational variations in 'The Mergency Man' and 'Dread' to substantive differences in 'Danny' and 'In Kerry'. Whether or not Yeats had anything to do with these changes, in Dun Emer and Cuala he continued his practice of revising the work he edited. Some authors affected were Æ, Katharine Tynan, Frank O'Connor and probably Oliver Gogarty. In most cases Yeats consulted with the authors about revisions.
73 'The Emergence of Synge' by George Roberts in *The Irish Times*. 1 August 1955. p. 5.
74 *Ibid*.
75 *J. M. Synge. Collected Works, I, Poems*, edited by Robin Skelton. London 1962. p. xxxvi.
76 *Selections from the Writings of Lord Dunsany*. Dublin 1912. n. pag.
77 *Certain Noble Plays of Japan*, edited by Ezra Pound. Dublin 1916. p. i.
78 *Ibid.*, p. ii.
79 *Ibid.*, p. xix.
80 *Ibid*.
81 Synge uses part of this analogy in his Preface to *The Tinker's Wedding*.
82 *The Irish Statesman*. 21 November 1925. p. 332.
83 *My Father's Son* by Frank O'Connor. New York 1969. p. 222.
84 *The Wild Bird's Nest*, poems translated by Frank O'Connor. Dublin 1932. pp. 14-5.
85 *The Permanence of Yeats*. New York, 1961. p. 330.
86 *Essays and Introductions* by W. B. Yeats. London, 1961, p. 497.
87 *The Identity of Yeats* by Richard Ellmann. London, 1954. p. 204.
88 *Broadsides* edited by W. B. Yeats and F. R. Higgins. Dublin, 1935. n. pag.

89 *Letters on Poetry from W. B. Yeats to Dorothy Wellesley* edited by Dorothy Wellesley. London, 1940. p. 150.
90 *Broadsides*, 1935. n. pag.
91 *Ibid.*
92 The revisions are in Yeats's hand in his own copy of Higgins's *The Dark Breed*. pp. 11-12. Quoted by permission. Yeats has crossed out the first stanza of the ballad, and it appears this way in *The Oxford Book of Modern Verse*, with the stanza intact in the 1935 *Broadsides*. Yeats probably made the revisions with both editions in mind; since Higgins was co-editor of the *Broadsides* he may have insisted on including the first stanza.
93 *Letters on Poetry.* p. 147.
94 *Far Have I Travelled* by Dorothy Wellesley. London, 1952. pp. 153-4.
95 *Dictionary of National Biography, 1951-1960.* p. 1041.
96 *Far Have I Travelled*, p. 58.
97 See the author's 'Yeats as Editor: Dorothy Wellesley's *Selections*' in *English Language Notes*. December 1973. pp. 112-18.
98 This poem was published originally in *A Broadside*, September 1937 in a version that still had three stanzas that Yeats had suggested she leave out. Yeats pleaded confusion and the corrected version appeared as an erratum in the bound *Broadsides* but missing the original illustration because Dorothy Wellesley thought it vulgar.
99 Foreword to *Broadsides*, 1935. Section II.
100 *Words for Music* by V. C. Clinton-Baddeley. Cambridge, 1941. p. 151.
101 *Letters on Poetry.* p. 100.
102 *Ibid.*, p. 102.
103 TS. Letter from Dorothy Wellesley to F. R. Higgins. 14 November 1938. MS. Collections. National Library of Ireland.
104 Most of the correspondence between Yeats and the Clarendon Press has been published by Jon Stallworthy in 'Yeats as Anthologist' in *In Excited Reverie*. London, 1965. pp. 171-92. Stallworthy also quotes extensively from Clarendon Press memoranda. The author has supplemented this where indicated.
105 Memorandum from Humphrey Milford to Kenneth Sisam. 15 October 1934. *Oxford Book* file. Clarendon Press. Quoted by permission.
106 *In Excited Reverie.* p. 174.
107 *Letters on Poetry.* pp. 20-1.
108 *Ah, Sweet Dancer, W. B. Yeats, Margot Ruddock, A Correspondence* edited by Roger McHugh. New York, 1971. p. 35.
109 *Letters on Poetry.* pp. 64-5.
110 *Ah, Sweet Dancer.* p. 42.
111 *In Excited Reverie.* p. 175.
112 Memo from Milford to R. W. Chapman. 8 November 1934. Clarendon Press file.

113 *In Excited Reverie.* p. 181.
114 *Ibid.*, p. 177.
115 *Ibid.*, p. 182.
116 *Letters on Poetry.* p. 40.
117 Though Yeats added some poems after this date, it is important to remember that Yeats had made the bulk of his selection by this time. At this point Auden's reputation rested almost entirely on his *Poems* (1930). (Yeats used the revised 1933 edition for his anthology.) Eliot had not yet published *Burnt Norton*. While Yeats did have his idiosyncrasies in making selections from these poets, he still did not have all the material of critics twenty years later.
118 Memo from Milford to Charles Williams. 4 May 1936. Clarendon Press file.
119 Copy of letter to A. P. Watt from Mrs. Yeats. 27 April 1936. Clarendon Press file. Letter from A. P. Watt to C. Williams. 16 June 1936. Clarendon Press file.
120 Introduction to *The Oxford Book of Modern Verse* edited by W. B. Yeats. London, 1936. pp. ix-xi. In subsequent references OBMV.
121 *Ibid.*, p. xvii.
122 *Ibid.*, p. xxvii.
123 *Essays and Introductions.* p. 499.
124 *OBMV.* p. xxv.
125 *Essays and Introductions.* p. 503.
126 *Ibid.*, p. 506.
127 *OBMV.* p. v.
128 *Letters on Poetry.* p. 91.
129 *Ibid.*, p. 81.
130 *Ibid.*, p. 127.
131 *In Excited Reverie.* p. 184.
132 *Letters on Poetry.* p. 64.
133 *Ibid.*, p. 126.
134 *OBMV.* p. xxi.
135 *Letters on Poetry.* p. 48.
136 *OBMV.* p. xxii.
137 These poems have been checked in the Contents and cut out from Yeats's own copy of *Personae* (1926). This was Yeats's method of preparing preliminary copy for the *Oxford Book*. The other poems originally selected were 'The Return', 'Ite', 'Yeux Glauques', 'South-Folk in Cold Country', 'Envoi' from *Hugh Selwyn Mauberley* and sections VII and XI from the same book.
138 *OBMV.* p. xxiv.
139 *Ibid.*, pp. xxv and xxxvi.
140 'The Public v. the Late Mr. William Butler Yeats', by W. H. Auden in *Partisan Review*. Spring 1939. p. 47.

141 A list Yeats sent to the Clarendon Press on 9 October 1935 indicated only three poems for Auden and three were printed in the first edition, but actually 'Before this loved one' had been run on as one poem with 'This lunar beauty', probably a copyist's mistake. After the first edition, the poems were printed separately as 368 and 368a.
142 *OBMV*. p. xviii.
143 *Wild Apples*. Dublin, 1930. n. pag.; *OBMV*. p. xxviii.
144 *DNB, 1951-60.* p. 1041.
145 *Essays and Introductions.* p. 507.
146 *Wild Apples.* n. pag.
147 Letter from W. B. Yeats to Clarendon Press. 4 September 1936. Clarendon Press file.
148 Revision in Yeats's personal copy of Pound's *Personae*. Quoted by permission.
149 *Kings, Lords, and Commons* by Frank O'Connor. New York, 1959. p. 100; *The Backward Look* by Frank O'Connor. London, 1967. p. 168; *Mourning Became Mrs. Spendlove* by Oliver Gogarty. New York, 1948. p. 223.
150 *Letters on Poetry.* p. 90.
151 *OBMV.* p. vii.
152 For Turner's comments on Yeats's revisions in his poems for the *Oxford Book*, see *The Arrow, W. B. Yeats Commemoration Number*. Summer 1939. pp. 18-19.
153 For the evidence for these revisions, see *English Language Notes*. December 1973. pp. 113-16.
154 Yeats has listed page numbers for nine poems by Nichols in his personal copy of *Ardours and Endurances*. London, 1917. These poems are all cut out which usually indicates an advanced state in Yeats's selecting process. This list includes two poems that clearly express an exultation in war, 'In the Grass : Halt by the Roadside' and 'Nearer'.
155 See for example *The Destructive Element* by Stephen Spender. London, 1935. pp. 130-1.
156 *Letters on Poetry.* p. 122.
157 *Ibid.*, p. 127.
158 Clarendon Press memo. *OBMV* file. 12 January 1951.

DATE DUE

HIGHSMITH 45-220